MW00996315

Daniel E. Edmonds

Start Small,

Do it Right,

Build it Strong!

Observing Jesus: What He Did That You Can Do

ISBN: 9798335298353

An Incite Publication

InciteMinistries.org

Edited By: Terri Edmonds and Lydia Edmonds Cobb
Artwork By: Blake Cobb

Printed By: Incite Publishing
Printed in the United States of America

First Printing Edition, 2024

I S B N 9798335298353

Dedication

This book is dedicated to:

My loving wife, Terri McSpedden Edmonds

My Parents – Bobby and Maie Edmonds

My Brother – David (and Venice) Edmonds

My Children and Grandchildren

Joshua and Lindsay Edmonds, Maya and Zoey

Lydia and Blake Cobb, Kinslee, Kennedy, Bryson, Elijah

To Alabama Disciple Making Movement Leaders:

Robert Mullins, Mark Gainey, Andy Frazier, Eric Taylor, Cody Hale,

Sarah Law, Marc Hodges, Glenn Sandifer, and Jay Gordon

To Faithful Disciple Making Partners:

Craig Etheredge and Ken Adams

To my Pastors and mentors:

Dr. Lawrence Phipps and Dr. Rick Lance

In Memory of Andrew L. Smith and Keith Edmonds

Acknowledging my encouragers with thanksgiving:

Jamie Baldwin, Eileen Mitchell, Steve Layton, Patty Burns, Belinda Stroud, Frank Jones

Charlotte Burgos, Julie Smith, Janet Eikenberry, Ramona Noah

Charles and Debe Rodgers and the Chisholm Baptist Church Family.

Table of Contents

AUTHOR'S PURPOSE

I was born in the Baptist Hospital, near to the Baptist Sunday School Board, located in the Baptist Holy Land of Nashville, Tennessee. The city is still there, the rest of us have departed. I say this to establish that I have observed Baptist life since birth and was on the Cradle Roll prior to my birth. I use the word *observe* because that is indicative of my nature. I am not a people person, as much as a people watcher. People fascinate me. Why do we do the things we do?

The more I observe, the more I question. A combination of questions I posed to myself and questions others have posed led me to write this book. I question statements I have heard through the years:

➢ We have an unchanging message, but ever-changing methodology. Is this statement true? Jesus came with unchanging truth and unchanging methodology that He intends for us to proclaim and imitate.

➢ Is there an answer to the age-old question, where do we get the leaders? No, but Jesus taught us how to avoid that question by making disciples.

➢ We have never done it that way before! This statement should cause us to move to the Word of God rather than the whims of society and traditions. If we have never done it His way before, then we have never done it right.

This is just a small sample, but it is that last statement that radically changed my approach to ministry. In collaborating with my pastor, Lawrence Phipps, on the book *Growing Sunday School TEAMS* (created in 1994 and now published through It's Life Ministry), I submitted the statement Start Small, Do It Right, Build It Strong, which had become my expression of the change that took place in my life as I studied Luke 5:1-11.

Start Small, Do It Right, Build It Strong went against my observations in the local church: we seem to Start Large, Do It For A While, Build It Down To The Ground, and Go Hunt Something New. We tend to want to lead masses and love the few who follow, whereas Jesus loved (had compassion) the masses but led the few. In leading the few, He demonstrated how to love the masses of all generations.

I have been privileged to serve in ministry since 1981. In 1996, I became a State Missionary for Alabama Baptists. No matter where I serve, the call remains the same: be a disciple who makes disciples that will make disciples. Occasionally, a remark is made that churches need to hear from practitioners. I still meet that qualification by living as a disciple to make disciples. That will be understood as you move through this book.

As I began my journey, I dreamed of the possibility that because of the work God did through me in disciple-making, even while I slept, someone I had discipled would lead another person across the world to become a follower of Christ. It was stunning how quickly that dream became a reality. I hope to encourage and equip you so that you may experience that reality in your life.

Terms like the Jesus model are being used today. I understand the desire to recreate the Jesus model of disciple-making. I am not bold enough to make that declaration. I will share observations from my investigation of the life of Jesus. My hope in sharing my observations is not to tear down what you are doing, but to help you evaluate everything, elevate the right things, and encourage you to do what God has called you to do: equip the saints!

CHAPTER 1

START SMALL, DO IT RIGHT, BUILD IT STRONG!

. . . LAUNCH OUT. . . LET DOWN THE NETS LUKE 5:4 KJV

A funny thing happened on the way to ministry: I discovered that not everyone thinks I am a genius. Would you believe people would question me? Momma did not tell me there would be days like this! Joking aside, we have all had frustrating days in ministry and will have more of them. What keeps me going? I have learned to be content in His call, constant in prayer, and continue in His Word. I will share with you the Bible passage that corrected my course, kept me going, and is the foundation for the motto that reminds me of how Jesus made disciples who grow generationally deep.

Observation 1: We have never done it that way before!

Luke's investigation helped shape my observations and applications of ministry. I began doing my own investigation of what I was observing in the church to see if there was more to the story. Like many ministers, I was often frustrated by what has been commonly referred to as the last words of the church: we have never done it that way before. Is there validity to the statement? Is there a way to overcome it? Did Jesus ever hear those words?

My investigation led me to Luke 5. Jesus was gaining notoriety in ministry. Though rejected in His hometown, He declared His mission to set the captive free. He began teaching with authority and power. He healed the sick including Simon Peter's mother-in-law. He cast out demons who recognized Him as the Son of God. He spent time in solitude and stayed focused on preaching the good news throughout Judea.

As chapter 5 unfolds, the crowds followed Him to the Lake of Gennesaret to hear Him preach. Two boats were there, at the edge of the water. Though working, the fishermen were engaged with the One they had heard in previous days. Simon allowed Jesus to teach from his boat, which was the least he could do to express appreciation for the Master. Then Jesus finished speaking and changed my view of ministry forever.

Jesus asked Simon to launch into the deep and let down the nets for a catch. Simon responded, *we have never done it that way before!* Now you and I know that is not exactly what he said, but it had the same meaning. What Jesus was asking went against everything they did when it came to fishing. They did not fish in the day. They did not fish in the deep. They were now mending and drying the nets. Why should they go against everything they knew about fishing? Only one reason: at Your Word.

It hit me like a bolt of lightning. Why should anyone think I know more about their church and practices than they do? Why do I know better than my predecessor? Why should they believe me over other consultants? Why? The truth is that they should not! It is not my church or my ministry; it is HIS! All of us should move at His Word, risking everything because we know it all belongs to Him. The fishermen gave up their lives (livelihood) and gained their lives. Launching out, Simon becomes Simon Peter, and the Master is recognized as Lord: new life, new identity, and His identity revealed. In this unmistakable life

4

changing event for Peter, wrecked by his sin, he is called to the Savior; follow Me and you will fish for people.

Like Peter, my life was dramatically changed. People should not move because I say so, but believers must move at His Word. From that moment of life-change onward, I determined to ask believers to do only what He said. Methodology must flow from Theology. Did I still hear those last words of the church? Yes, but I had a foundation for a better response: if we have never done it this way before, then it is time we do! His way is best. He is <u>the</u> way.

Observation 2: He is <u>the</u> Way.

The masses had gathered on the shore to hear His teaching and see a miracle performed by Jesus. Most people today are on the shore or away from Jesus. When the masses would gather, Jesus would have compassion and teach them about the Kingdom. Yet, we often see Him slipping away from the masses to spend time with a few. The few were in the boat with Him that day when He challenged them by commanding and sending them to the deep. Jesus went from gathering the masses, to the grouping of a few, to guiding them into the deep waters of fishing for people.

This too became a radical altering of my mindset in ministry. If I wanted to stay true to His word, I needed the discipline to **start small, do it right, build it strong.** Jesus loved the masses but led the few to reach the masses for generations in the future. In church life, we want to lead the masses and love the few who do what we ask. I refer to our current strategy as start large, grow it to the ground, start over with a new program. Jesus' method will produce generational depth as opposed to rapid growth toward steady decline.

Observation 3: Start Small.

If anyone in history could have led the masses, it was Jesus. However, in Luke 5, we see him starting small. In fact, by the end of the chapter He had only five disciples, including Andrew. By chapter 6, He forms a small group. If you want to change the culture, build disciples to be commissioned as disciple-makers: start small. I will spend more time on this topic in later chapters, but please note in Luke 5 the purpose of the group was to fish for people.

Observation 4: Do It Right.

In Luke's follow up book, Acts, he addresses Theophilus and summarizes the previous book by saying he recorded all that Jesus had done and taught. I was curious about the ordering of the words, do and teach, only to discover that was THE teaching method to be utilized by everyone (Deuteronomy 6). However, clearly those occupying the seat of Moses had moved away from proper methodology. Why? Bad theology. Their theology was so bad that a new convert would become "twice as much a child of hell as you are" (Matthew 23:15 NIV).

What if next Sunday you could teach only the things you do? Would that change your lesson plan? People know, intuitively, whether you do what you teach. We need to be "doers of the word, and not hearers only" (James 1:22). Jesus did what He taught. He went to the deep water with them to show them the power and authority of His word. Even though astonished by what had taken place, they had no doubt that He could guide them to fish for people. Teaching is about imitation and information. More people learn from the imitation of those who do and teach. Paul said, imitate me as I imitate Christ so others might be saved (1 Corinthians 10:33 – 11:1 NKJV).

Observation 5: Build it strong.

Again, our temptation is to build it quickly. Jesus invested heavily in the lives of the disciples to build it strong throughout time. He did not give them the five easy steps to being a disciple-maker. He did not move them through a program or process. Instead, He poured His life into them. He modeled. He molded. He moved them to do as He had done. Fully trained, they would be like Him (Luke 6:40). He could commission them because they had gone with Him to become like Him: a disciple-maker.

Observation 6: Identity and Authority are keys in disciple-making.

In my evaluation of the book *Cultivate Disciplemaking,* I applauded the authors Kevin Blackwell and Randy Norris for addressing two critical issues in disciple-making: identity and authority. Luke 5 spoke volumes to me on these concerns. Immediately, upon calling the fishermen, Jesus established His messianic identity by healing the leper. In chapter 4 of Luke, Jesus pointed out many in Israel had leprosy in the time of Elisha, but only Naaman was cleansed by God. Only one Jew had ever been cleansed of leprosy, Miriam. Both people with leprosy had been cleansed by God. Jews knew that only God could cleanse leprosy. They were certain that you became a person with leprosy because of your overwhelming sin, and only the Leper Messiah of Isaiah 53 could touch and cleanse a person with leprosy. Our overwhelming sin can be cleansed only by the Messiah. Jesus is the Messiah, and He demonstrated that vividly for all in the aftermath of the fishermen leaving everything behind.

Jesus further demonstrated His identity and authority by forgiving the sin and healing the crippled body of one brought by faith to Jesus. Disciples know the identity and authority of Jesus and demonstrate this by bringing the hopeless and helpless to Him. They fish for people, even the most hated of people. I always marveled that tax collectors were in a category of their own in the minds of Jewish leaders (5:30). May we not be guilty of the same condemnation but recognize everyone needs Jesus.

We leave Luke chapter 5 on a sad note. Not everyone will follow Jesus. Some will still believe the old way is better. However, this is an essential note for what I will share going forward in this book. For some, they do not want to change, preferring the old way though it will not bear fruit that remains. Not everyone will move at His word (abide) and launch out into the deep (obey) to become disciples who will make disciples for generations to come.

Looking Ahead.

This book has three sections with multiple chapters. The three sections are

1. Growing Up as a Disciple.
2. Groups that Multiply.
3. Guiding a Movement of Multiplying Disciples.

Each chapter affords you the opportunity to process your thoughts and to develop a plan.

YOUR OBSERVATIONS

1. As you have read, what is the Big Idea from this chapter?

2. What is the Bright Idea that has you thinking?

3. What is the Better Idea that you will implement?

START SMALL, DO IT RIGHT, BUILD IT STRONG

SECTION 1

GROWING UP AS A DISCIPLE

CHAPTER 2

BEGINNINGS, LAYING DOWN THE MARKERS

IN THE BEGINNING GENESIS 1:1, JOHN 1:1.

Beginnings are important. God is the author and the authority in whom we find purpose and identity. My life began in a mission church. I cannot overstate how important that beginning has been for my life. The church started small, and Terri and I started small (preschoolers). I will share some of what we learned about becoming disciples and being disciple-makers on the path of the unfolding story and the unfinished work.

How much can I remember of my time in preschool? Honestly, not much though what I remember is significant for understanding the foundational work of making disciples. I remember that through scripture, stories, and songs, I was taught what I call Gospel basics. Sooner or later, every disciple needs the pure spiritual milk of the Word. Sooner, meaning as a preschooler, is best, so I was blessed.

The second thing I remember was my dad taking me to the church house on Sunday morning to prepare the farmhouse and cinder block building for Sunday School and Worship. The most memorable part of this venture was, on many Sunday mornings, having to chase the 'possum family out of the farmhouse basement so that young adults could meet for Sunday School.

I still tell people that my first job in Sunday School was chasing 'possums, and it is still my job. A 'possum is an animal that can appear dead, even though it is very much alive. Welcome to Sunday School! In Sunday School, we take what is so alive, the Word of God, and (often) make it appear to the rest of the world as though it is dead.

My dad could have done the job faster without me, but he took me to teach me that God will always have a work He wants to do through me. This became the methodology of the children's ministry. They still taught the Word, but they began taking us to see the Word at work in the world. Leaders took me to do mission work, make visits, and many other ministry experiences. They led out in the work but allowed me to help and to learn through observation and participation.

The next phase of growth was as I became a teenager. I was still being taught Gospel truth and taken on mission/ministry experiences, but now they added training me to take the lead. By the time I was sixteen, I served as the director of a Mission Vacation Bible School and taught adult Sunday School, as well as used my gifts in the Worship Service. Do not misunderstand, the adult was still present, but the role reversed, and I was leading while they observed and encouraged.

My wife has similar experiences, so it was no surprise that as we became adults, we sought opportunities to serve. Those wonderful leaders did not invest in us so that we could sit on the sidelines the rest of our lives. They were glad to see the fruit of their labor as they turned us loose to serve in our areas of giftedness.

The sad reality is that fewer people in the following generations had this experience of growth from preschooler to adulthood. However, if people are to become disciples, non-believers or new believers of any age will need to be **taught** Gospel basics, **taken** to learn how to do missions and ministry, and

trained to become disciples who make disciples of all nations.

YOUR OBSERVATIONS

1. Beginnings are important. When, where, and at what age did your journey/story begin?

2. As you have read, what is your Big Idea from this chapter?

3. What is the Bright Idea that has you thinking?

4. What is the Better Idea that you will implement?

CHAPTER 3

MARKERS TO MOVEMENT

. . . EVERYONE FULLY TRAINED WILL BE LIKE THEIR TEACHER LUKE 6:40 NIV

Numerous pastors and leaders have explained the importance of milk and meat in Scripture. Clearly, Paul and the writer of Hebrews urged growth from milk to meat. In conferences, I often ask people to express their thoughts about milk in Scripture. The common responses are that milk is foundational truth and encouragement from the Word. I do not argue their expressions but point to a reality that my pastor, Lawrence Phipps, pointed out to me: milk must be given (see the passages in 1 Corinthians 3 and Hebrews 5). Just like a mother must provide a newborn nourishment, a newborn believer must be given pure spiritual milk. There is a growth process for babies and new believers that cannot be bypassed. (Note: milk is not about content, but conduit. Theologically rich sermons are still <u>given</u> to the recipient). You will always need the spiritual milk of the Word. This milk is essential to the health of disciples throughout their lives.

I have watched my children and grandchildren move through this process from milk to solid food given to them, to feeding themselves with a spoon (hand), then graduating to using a fork and knife. Finally, they achieve independence by mastering the art of eating. One could say that when children are fully mature, they become like their teacher. Though milk and meat build strength, there is much more to becoming an imitator of Christ.

In the previous chapter, I talked about beginnings and the markers that revealed progress toward becoming a disciple who is serving through the gifting of the Spirit. As I stated, for Terri and me, this happened through relationships and ministries (programs) of the church. However, our culture has changed dramatically. In the 1980's, we moved to a 24/7 society, and many of the ministries that we leaned into are no longer available or effective due to the lifestyles of those engaged. This resulted in our churches moving only a small percentage of people past the milk and/or meat markers. Milk is dispensed in gatherings, and groups give participants the opportunity to dig into the Word (meat) and learn to feed themselves. Assimilation can be achieved by getting people in worship, a group, and serving. However, this is not adequate for making a disciple who will become a disciple-maker.

Jesus is the Master teacher, and we, when fully trained, should imitate Him. This will require more than milk and meat. I would suggest to you that we need to look at Jesus' methodology in growing His followers into disciples who would make disciples. In addition to milk and meat, I see him model (do and teach), engage His disciples in missions (send), call them to multiply (fruitfulness), and commission them into the movement He started. It is a movement of imitation, so milk and meat are always needed for strength and stamina. Likewise, you never quit modeling, leave the mission field, or cease to multiply.

I worked for United Parcel Service for six years, finishing my tenure as a Hub Supervisor. I left because of God's call on my life in ministry. Early in my time at Seminary, a professor asked me about my experience at UPS. He specifically wanted to know about my knowledge of how they trained their people since they were known for their effectiveness in training. When I shared with him that my job was to train employees, he asked if I could take what UPS did and apply it to the local church. At first, I laughed at him, which was not the best thing to do. I explained the reason I laughed was that I found UPS's training to be modeled after the methodology of Jesus with the disciples.

As an example of the training, I often trained people to load a truck. This may sound simple, but there is a right way of doing it. When done correctly, there are more packages in the truck, which means fewer trucks on the road and more money in profit. In that day, as a supervisor, I had to wear a suit. I would take new employees into a forty-five-foot-long trailer with a temperature often exceeding one hundred degrees. I would leave the employees near the opening and allow them simply to observe. After a few minutes, I would tell them the basics (milk) of the job as they continued to watch. I explained every move I made, where my eyes should be, and how I made sure only correct packages were loaded.

In the next phase, I invited the employees to come along side and help. This time was still heavy on instruction for me, but they participated as I instructed. A subtle change was I began to engage them in conversation: Where should you be looking? Why did you make that move? Where should you load that box? Have you built a strong foundation? The employees could ask questions too.

As their answers became more satisfactory, I moved into the collaboration phase. In this step, the roles reversed in that they took the lead, and I helped them. They would do most of the talking and instructing while I would assist and follow (correct) instructions.

Finally, I would move toward the opening; they would do the work, and I would evaluate. Occasionally, I would do something to test their accuracy and ability. The amount of time for this process was different for each employee. The time was reduced with any prior experience, cross-training, and willingness to learn.

In a similar experience, a fellow supervisor came to me for help. He explained that his career up to that point was on the unloading end of the operation. However, now he was to train employees to load trucks. He asked me to teach him saying, "I cannot teach them until I can do what I am teaching." There is a great message for the church in his statement.

I cherish my time at United Parcel Service. In that experience, I discovered that Jesus' methodology works everywhere in life. Additionally, I had never experienced disciple-making with an adult that was a new believer. UPS helped me see the pattern for adults that was taught and modeled by Jesus.

At this point, without excessive commentary, I want to share the outline that I have shared for many years that reflects what I learned growing up and what I experienced on the job. The outline does not stop with multiplication. Multiplication is not the goal or the finish line for a disciple. Eugene Peterson described being a disciple as movement: *A Long Obedience In The Same Direction.* It is a movement of imitating Christ by emptying self, humbly abiding, and completely obeying until death. This is the movement to which we are called by Christ in the Great Commission.

TEACHING OUTLINE FROM MILK TO MOVEMENT

From Milk to Meat: Move from hearing to reading: Observation Phase:

(I do, You watch)

1. Like newborn babies, crave pure spiritual milk, so that by it you may grow up in your salvation, now that you have tasted that the Lord is good. 1 Peter 2:2 – 3

2. Brothers and sisters, I could not address you as people who live by the Spirit but as people who are still worldly—mere infants in Christ. I gave you milk, not solid food, for you were not yet ready for it. Indeed, you are still not ready. You are still worldly. For since there is jealousy and quarreling among you, are you not worldly? Are you not acting like mere humans? 1 Corinthians 3:1 – 3

3. We have much to say about this, but it is hard to make it clear to you because you no longer try to understand. In fact, though by this time you ought to be teachers, you need someone to teach you the elementary truths of God's word all over again. You need milk, not solid food! Hebrews 5: 11 – 12

How do you receive milk? By hearing.

From Meat to Model: Move from reading to applying: Participation Phase:

(I do, You help)

1. Study to show thyself approved unto God, a workman who needeth not to be ashamed, rightly dividing the word of truth. 2 Timothy 2:15

2. In my former book, Theophilus, I wrote about all that Jesus began to do and to teach. Acts 1:1

3. "Come, follow me," Jesus said, "and I will send you out to fish for people." Mark 1:17

From Model to Mission: **Move from studying to doing:**   **Collaboration Phase:**

(You do, I help)

1. Calling the Twelve to him, he began to send them out two by two and gave them authority over impure spirits. These were his instructions: "Take nothing for the journey except a staff—no bread, no bag, no money in your belts. Wear sandals but not an extra shirt. Whenever you enter a house, stay there until you leave that town. And if any place will not welcome you or listen to you, leave that place and shake the dust off your feet as a testimony against them." Mark 6:7 – 11

2. The apostles gathered around Jesus and reported to him all they had done and taught. Mark 6:30

From Mission to Multiply: **Move from doing to becoming a disciple:**   **Evaluation Phase:**

(You do, I watch)

1. God blessed them and said to them, "Be fruitful and increase in number; fill the earth and subdue it. Rule over the fish in the sea and the birds in the sky and over every living creature that moves on the ground." Genesis 1:28

2. Therefore, go and make disciples of all nations, baptizing them in the name of the Father and of the Son and of the Holy Spirit, and teaching them to obey everything I have commanded you. And surely I am with you always, to the very end of the age." Matthew 28:19 – 20

Multiplication Phase: **Move from being a disciple to disciple-maker:**

(You do & teach).

Multiplication is the desire of most churches. However, there is a greater call on our lives: abide and obey to become a guide in the disciple-making movement.

Movement Creation: **Make disciple-makers until He comes:**

Having gone, now go!

More will be said about this later, but few churches seek to facilitate this movement that results in new groups and new gatherings beyond the walls of the church.

(Years after leaving UPS, I discovered that Mike Breen, *Building a Discipling Culture,* expressed this idea for the church in what has become known as the Disciples Square. His wording is above in the parenthetical notes).

Additional thoughts:

Milk

In the previous chapter it was mentioned that this marker coincides with preschool ministry or to a non-believer or new believer of any age. One complaint I often receive about Sunday School curriculum is that it is not very deep. However, the Sunday School curriculum is to enable movement from milk to meat, and a properly led group will include modeling and mission opportunities. The key is not the curriculum, but the person called to guide the process.

A few tips:

- Realize that those needing milk are at first dependent on you to speak, sing, and share the Word.

- Repetition is a friend to this step in the process.

- Like a preschooler, a non-believer or new believer should be allowed to ask the questions. The *why* question must be answered alongside of the *who* and *what* questions.

- Many in this stage will choose to attend worship only until a trust relationship is built with a group leader.

- Assume nothing, avoid phrases like we all know or have heard this story.

- Encourage learning to use the Bible. Introduce them to the table of contents by having all group members turn to it before going to the assigned passage. Use this as a time to teach the books of the Bible.

- The primary teaching methodology at this stage is lecture but moves toward engaging the learner in reading and interacting with the concepts being taught.

Meat

This is the time to begin asking the learner to come alongside of you to learn how to unearth the truth of God's Word and apply it to their lives. At this point, you begin to ask them questions and even give them tasks to accomplish.

A few tips:

- I developed HEART to engage all believers and non-believers in getting the meat of the Word by learning to apply and share what they learn: Highlight, Express, Ask, Relate to Life, Tell Someone (See Appendix).

- Ask learners to share what they discovered and ask questions using the HEART method to Bible study.

- Do not fear questions. You will be able to answer every question, though sometimes the answer may be "I don't know." This answer is golden because it is the invitation to study together and find truth and application to life.

- Specifically see if learners know someone that needs to hear what they have learned. Build good disciplines into the process.

- The primary teaching methodology at this stage is a mix of methodologies to encourage discussion and engaging in application of concepts. Remember, the learners ask the best discussion questions not the guide.

Model

Remember when you were young and were taught to tie your shoes? How did it happen? Did your dad bring you into a room with a dozen other children and lecture you on the fine art of shoe tying? Did your mom take you to watch a documentary on tying shoes? Did someone come alongside you and take you through the process? In other words, did they take you aside and model the behavior, then involve you in the behavior until you mastered the subject? I remember my parents coming alongside, demonstrating on their shoe while talking through the steps (bunny ears story), and asking me to mimic their steps until I mastered shoe tying. We then celebrated as I demonstrated what I learned for others. How effective was this modeling? I still remember how to tie my shoes and can teach others.

Whether in Deuteronomy 6:1, Matthew 28:19-20, or Acts 1:1, the Bible is clear that we teach obedience by modeling the behavior. Another way to think of this is on the job training, like I did at UPS.

My home church engaged me in numerous ministries by partnering me with someone who would demonstrate and teach me exactly what I needed to do. Ministries included mission projects, wiring the new sanctuary for sound, sealing the church parking lot, hospital and outreach visits, etc. Prior to engaging in these activities, I only knew that I was part of the body of Christ, and I was created in Christ to serve. My pastor often said to me, "show up and we will show you how." Honestly, I was often clueless as to what to do (prior to going) or even if it were something I would ever want to do again. The benefit of going was discovering how God would use me in the future.

A few tips:

- Do not skip a step. It is important to supply milk and meat before modeling behavior. Theology and philosophy are essential to methodology. Supply the *why* and *what* before moving to *how*.

- To model a behavior does not mean that you have perfected it, but that you practice it consistently.

- Model ministries that are age-appropriate for involvement.

- Modeling is not doing the work for them but equipping them to do the work.

- The primary teaching methodology at this stage is commonly called On the Job Training (UPS) or the Disciples' Square (Breen).

Mission: having experienced the Word in action, train them for the mission.

By this time, the believers should have been involved in a variety of ministries. This engagement along with spiritual gift discovery should enable them to see how God might use them going forward. Train them specifically for a task they are drawn to and are passionate about doing. This will require someone in the same ministry area mentoring them.

A few tips:

- Spiritual Gift inventories should be utilized in this step.

- The best inventories include meeting with a coach to interpret and discover ministry matches.

- Encourage short-term experiences so that the individual may affirm and be affirmed in ministry.

- The primary teaching methodology at this stage is a mix of observation, instruction, encouragement, and celebration.

Multiplication

Most churches want to see multiplication, primarily in groups. The problem is churches multiply groups without making disciples. Leaders measure success by followers (keeping people in seats). Disciples view success in multiplication (sending people out).

A few tips:

- LifeWay correctly stated that Groups Matter, but the disciple in the group matters more. We all have people leading groups that do not seek to multiply and whose model/style of teaching is not reproducible.

- Organize groups to multiply. Constant multiplication should be the stated goal of any new group. This requires a reproducible model focused on reaching people and developing disciples who can replicate the experience of moving people from milk to meat to model to mission to multiply.

- Personally, I like the TEAMS model (*Growing Sunday School TEAMS*) along with the Peter, James, and John model of Jesus (See Appendix). My friend, Steve Layton, utilizes the GroupLIFE model (makingdisciplesal.org). Others have used the Reach, Teach, and Minister model to organize a class for effective multiplication.

Movement Guide

This will become the topic in the latter portion of this book. I hope you discover it as an 'ah-ha' moment of the disciple-making movement. It is not a process or lifestyle disciple-making. It is discovering your identity by stepping into the unfinished work of the Great Commission, making disciples of all nations until He comes. The Great Commission is no longer what you do, it defines who you are until He comes.

A final thought on United Parcel Service and making disciples will serve to challenge us all. As a result of the Jesus methodology that I utilized, very often one of my very best employees would be promoted. One day, the Area Manager asked how that made me feel, and I responded, "complimented." The manager was stunned by my answer thinking that I would be angry. Most supervisors did not want to lose their best workers, but I wanted them to grow and go on to bigger, better things.

The manager decided to put my methodology to the test. He invited (ordered) me to go with him to the breakroom. He wanted to see if my area would continue to operate at peak efficiency without my physical presence. During the hour we were together, many aspects of the operation that are normally done only by a supervisor would occur. If there was any breakdown in operations, we would hear it announced. We heard announcements about many areas, but none pertaining to mine. In my absence, the employees stepped into my role as needed. They called at the appropriate times for changes in trailers, filled out the paperwork with the appropriate security seals, and did everything that I would have done. Fully trained, they had become like their teacher. When opportunities came, they were ready to be sent.

When you make disciples, God will call them according to His will and pleasure. Feel complimented when they hear the call of God on their lives and become the next chapter of the unfolding story in the unfinished work.

Group leaders often complained, "why do you always come and get my best people." My response, "I did not. God did. You should feel complimented that they are responding to His call on their life because of the work God did through you." Additional thought, why would God want your worst or less than the best people?

YOUR OBSERVATIONS

1. Helping people grow to become disciples is essential. Do you have groups designed to help people move from milk to multiplication?

2. Are your group leaders more satisfied with getting people in seats or sending them into service by starting new groups? What do you celebrate, seating capacity or sending capacity?

3. What is your Big Idea from this chapter?

4. What is the Bright Idea that has you thinking?

5. What is the Better Idea that you will implement?

CHAPTER 4
ALIGNING WITH THE WINNER

JESUS IS THE CORNERSTONE AND THE FOUNDATION THAT HAS BEEN LAID EPHESIANS 2:20 AND 1 CORINTHIANS 3:11.

Warning, this chapter may be painful to read. I have shared the unfolding story that God in His love has granted me. I have reflected on what God has shown me through His Word and revealed to me through His disciples who were willing to start small (with me), do it right, build me strong until He called me into the unfinished work of the Great Commission. His call led me to become a State Missionary in June of 1996. It has been a blessing to come alongside churches in Alabama and throughout the country. During this time, I along with others have noticed that the church has been in decline. In this chapter, I want to address the current reality of many churches across the land and answer the question: what happened?

All the following are true stories. Each has happened in whole or part in numerous churches. They represent the most common experiences through my years as a State Missionary and as the perennial guest in groups. Confessionally, I never help the group out in how to greet, treat, or seat a guest. I do not introduce myself as a minister or missionary in hopes of avoiding special treatment.

No one noticed when I walked in the room because they were preoccupied with getting snacks, coffee, and talking to each other. I made my way toward the seats but noticed most were reserved by a Bible, book, coat, or purse. On the front row (no surprise), I found an unclaimed seat. Only one other person was seated, also on the front row though on the other side of the aisle. After a few minutes, he got up and walked over to me. He said, "I am tired of sitting there waiting for someone to greet me." He shared his name and told me it was his first time to be in the group. I know he was thinking I might be embarrassed because I did not greet him but imagine his shock when I told him that I was also a first-time guest. The story gets worse but suffice it to say I was sitting in an inward focused group.

The next story involves a men's group that did a good job of making me feel welcomed and included. As they took prayer request, they let me know if the individual was a member of the group or someone that was a friend. As I listened to the requests, they mentioned a group member who was in the hospital as of their last gathering. The leader asked for an update, but no one knew his status. Finally, one member explained that he saw the church hospital board on the way to the group. The member was no longer listed, so he must have gone home. I realized I was sitting in a group that would pray about anything but did not minister beyond the meeting time.

In the final story, Terri and I were greeted by a staff member that recognized me. He confirmed my identity and then asked my wife and I our ages. We were both thirty-eight (recent story), and he had a group for couples thirty-eight to thirty-nine years old. I was shocked. I had never age-graded to such a small span of years. When we got to the group, we recognized what we already knew; people will lie about their age. Most people in that group were past forty-five years of age. Undaunted, we made our way to empty seats, and my wife asked the couple if we could sit by them. The response was that they had friends that would come, so they pointed to seats where no one ever sat. I immediately knew why no one would sit in those seats, your back was to everyone else in the room. We took our seats, and when it was time to begin, a group member announced, "The teacher is late, again, but if he doesn't show up in ten minutes, we will just muddle through the best we can." He did eventually arrive, but the story only got worse. I wish I could say that was the most dysfunctional group ever, but it became a common occurrence. Other friends have related their own similar experience of being a guest.

The common thread among the classes? The teaching time was primarily a lecture to people not interested in building biblical community. Additionally, when my children were young, they would share their experiences of eating snacks and playing games with no connection to the Bible.

In conferences, the common questions are 1) how do you get teachers to be on time? 2) how do you get groups to minister effectively? 3) how do you get group members to participate? 4) how do you get groups to be outward focused? 5) how do you get group members to attend more frequently? The summary of all the questions: what has happened to us (as a Church, Sunday School, or Group)?

To help conferees analyze their situation, I ask them to respond to the following scenario: I am a friend that you would like to come to your group (Sunday School); tell me about it. I have received more than forty responses in a matter of ten minutes, though rarely do I hear anything about outreach, missions, or disciple-making. After they tell me everything they can, I ask them to tell me what of those things I will experience if I attend. Without fail, they reduce the list to three things: Fellowship, Prayer, and the Lesson/Bible teaching. No wonder most of our groups are thought of as Bible study fellowships.

If Bible study fellowship is the common descriptor, then let us analyze the reality of the group time.

Fellowship

I ask conferees, how long does fellowship time last, and the range is five to fifteen minutes. I then ask what happens in those fifteen minutes, and usually it has something to do with snacks and a conversation with a close friend. Fellowship does not focus on guests, nor does it serve a purpose other than waiting for everyone to arrive (including the teacher). In other words, we waste time. Fellowship time ends when someone says, "Looks like everybody is here, so let's get started." I am for fellowship, but it needs to come before the actual start time, and group members should be present with the expectation of greeting guests. The current reality exposes the lack of outreach in our groups since they do not expect guests.

Prayer

When fellowship time is over and the group gets started, they begin with prayer requests. This can be an uncomfortable time of over-sharing information and sometimes, gossip. I tease my doctor friends about wasting time in medical school: If they had gone to Sunday School, they would know about every disease and how to cure it. Prayer requests can take ten to twenty minutes and concludes with a minute-long prayer where, now that God has been informed, we ask Him to do something about it (sarcasm, I know). Rarely are any ministry or outreach assignments made because of our prayer focus.

Bible Teaching

Finally, it is time to teach the lesson. That phrase, teach the lesson, has never been a goal of Sunday School. It makes me feel uncomfortable. When somebody tells me they are going to teach me a lesson, it is not usually a good thing. Also, the target is getting through the lesson, not teaching me the Bible.

Finally, the test is on the teacher: Did he get through the lesson, or did he run out of time?

The dominant teaching methodology today is lecturing. There are some variations that include reading the leader's guide and leading a discussion of curriculum prescribed questions. The burden of preparation for these methodologies is on the teacher. Only the teacher must prepare for Sunday morning. However, the spiritual growth of students will be limited unless they are actively engaged in preparing for and participating in the Bible study.

The goal should be to teach people the Bible so that their lives can be transformed. The only way you can teach people is to know them and where they are on the milk to multiplication continuum. Transformation takes place when the teaching comes from one who is being transformed by the Word and the group members are engaging in personal Bible study and application of the Word through evangelism, missions, and ministry.

Disciples are not made by taking them deep in the Word (only) but getting them wide with the Word by going as a disciple into their Jerusalem, Judea, Samaria, and ends of the earth. This leads to how I answer the question of what has happened to us. My simple answer, we have lost our *why*. Steve Layton includes that we have lost our *why*, our *way*, and our *work*. This is the whole truth of the current reality.

Our *Why*

Matthew 22 contains the Great Commandment. Jesus was asked to identify the greatest commandment, and He responded, "Love the Lord your God with all your heart and with all your soul and with all your mind. This is the first and greatest commandment. And the second is like it: Love your neighbor as yourself. All the Law and the Prophets hang on these two commandments" (Matthew 22:37-40 NIV).

Loving God and loving people is not a feeling. It is an action. It defines the essence of why we are here: to Love Him with all our being and to love others in the same manner as we love ourselves. In groups, we spend our time focused on content rather than focusing on how to live and obey biblical content as we love Him and others. We need to be transformed to live as Christ, to obey the Word: not just hearers, but doers (James 1:22).

Our *Way*

The Great Commission of Matthew 28 is the Way we obey the Word. Often, we think of the Great Commission as what we do, but it is Who we are: people of the Way as we love Him and love others. Jesus is the Way, and we are ambassadors of the Way by being disciples who make disciples of all nations until He comes.

Our *Work*

All disciples are to live as salt and light in this world. However, Christ has given some to the church to equip the saints (Ephesians 4). This Great Call has marked my life throughout ministry. I, like many ministers, often find myself doing the work **for** saints and calling that ministry. Delegation is hard for many, but we are to do more than delegate. We are to equip His people until they grow unified in faith, mature in Him, speak truth in love, and do their part of the unfinished work of the Great Commission.

Our *why, way,* and *work* combine to enable us to become true image bearers, obedient to His authority with our identity in Christ, and to be ambassadors of Christ as God makes His appeal through us (2 Corinthians 5:20).

Transformational teaching leads others to discover themselves in the unfolding story of God's redeeming love and the unfinished work of the Great Commandment, Great Commission, and the Great Call.

A few tips for current groups:

Fellowship

- Fellowship time should begin 15 minutes before group/class time.

- Develop a list of people that your group members desire to be in the group.

- Create numerous fellowships outside of the group to connect members to prospective members.

- Come early with the expectation that guests will attend.

- Use fellowship time to gather prayer requests and for an icebreaker activity.

Prayer

- Enlist a Prayer Ministry Leader who will gather prayer requests during fellowship time or through care group leaders during the week.

- Utilize prayer list to make ministry assignments.

- The Prayer Ministry Leader will read the prayer list (no commentary) and pray to begin the class.

Lesson (Teach People the Bible)

- Teach people the Bible for life change. The objective is not to get through a lesson, but to engage people in hearing and doing God's Word.

- Involve people prior to the study by giving them simple assignments. For example, give them a question to ponder during the week so that they will be prepared to respond. Ask someone to be prepared to read the Scripture.

Sunday School and Small Group attendance will increase with involvement. Invest in their lives and involve them in biblical community. No one wants to be an outsider or spectator. People will value a group that places value on them.

YOUR OBSERVATIONS

1. Reflect on this chapter. Do you have groups that have lost their *Why*? Their *Way*? Their *Work*?

2. Are your groups organized to allow maximum participation inside and outside the group meeting time?

3. As you have read, what is your Big Idea from this chapter?

4. What is the Bright Idea that has you thinking?

5. What is the Better Idea that you will implement?

CHAPTER 5

EXAM TIME

WHAT YOU ARE DOING IS NOT GOOD EXODUS 18:17

From the time of Moses, groups have been important in Scripture. Jesus started a group to make disciples in Matthew 4. To feed the five thousand, Jesus had the disciples put people in groups. The Acts 2 church caught the model Jesus taught and groups multiplied. What about your groups? Are they open to new people? Are they overcrowded? Are they stagnant? Is your worship service growing, but your groups are not multiplying? It is examination time.

I met with a church that was ecstatic about the new people coming into Worship. People were being saved, being baptized, and bringing their friends. At the same time, their groups were not growing or multiplying. Those being saved were not going to Sunday School or Small groups. Worship attendance was more than double the number in groups. They understood the importance of a group strategy to make disciples. If they could not get the new members in a group, they would not grow spiritually to become a maturing disciple.

I listened as they excitedly talked about a recent convert who was bringing friends every Sunday. Many of his friends were being saved and baptized. While I listened, I discerned the approximate age of this new convert and realized his potential teacher was at the table with us. I looked at this teacher and asked if my suspicions were accurate. He affirmed my conclusion. In jest, I shared that State Missionaries were all given magic dust that would cause people to go to Sunday School the following Sunday. With that statement, I asked, "If I do that, how will that work out?" The teacher hung his head and responded, "Not well."

The leader began to explain his answer in two parts. First, it would not work because his current members had been together for quite some time. New people would be greeted, but they would not feel like they belonged unless they had a willingness to "stick it out for many months." The second reason hurt him personally. He said, "My teaching is aimed at those in the group and would go over the head of a new believer or non-believer."

This teacher properly analyzed his class and most groups in churches today. The hallmark of group life centers around relationships and Bible study. The longer the group exists, the closer people grow in relationships and the deeper they go in their understanding of the Word of God. While these two elements are good for those in the group, they tend to exclude those outside of it. The closer the fellowship, the more difficult it is for an outsider to penetrate the inner circle to gain a sense of belonging. The deeper the Bible Study, the harder it is for someone new to the group to understand and participate. The outcome is that groups are no longer accessible to newcomers after they have existed eighteen months to two years.

These leaders readily embraced the idea that new groups must be formed to give opportunity for these new believers to grasp the Word, to mature as believers, and to build relationships with others in the church. However, they shared how they had tried to get people to leave their group to start new groups.

It just did not work. Then a revelation came to them. They realized that the current leader was usually the one to raise someone up to care for the existing group while they moved on to start new ones, for example, Paul and Timothy (2 Timothy 2:2). Within a year, their group attendance doubled.

I have conducted informal surveys to discover that the majority of adult Sunday School attenders have been in Sunday School since early childhood. Typically, I discover that the church has few, if any, adults in attendance who have been in Sunday School less than two years. I encourage church leadership to conduct a similar assessment to reveal the effectiveness of the Sunday School in assimilating new believers.

YOUR OBSERVATIONS

1. How many new groups were started within the last two years in your church?

2. Are you struggling to find new teachers?

3. As you have read, what is your Big Idea from this chapter?

4. What is the Bright Idea that has you thinking?

5. What is the Better Idea that you will implement?

CHAPTER 6

SECTION CLOSING THOUGHTS

WE ARE HIS WORKMANSHIP, CREATED IN CHRIST JESUS FOR GOOD WORKS . . . THAT WE SHOULD

WALK IN THEM EPHESIANS 2:10 ESV

I am daily overwhelmed by 1 Corinthians 6:19-20. I am not my own; I have been blood bought to honor God. This is not my story; it is His story that I have entered by His grace. In Christ, I am created for good works to walk in them. If life were a swimming pool and was all about me, I would not get in over my head. I would stay in my comfort zone because of fear. My comfort zone is a prison that prevents me from experiencing the blessings that God has in store – His unfolding story of grace. In the unfolding story, I stay in over my head relying on Him alone. Staying in the deep end keeps me focused on the One who is the Hero, the Rescuer, and the Creator of good works. He has designed these works for me so that I may glorify Him by walking in them.

Fellow laborers, you may be experiencing the feeling of being in the deep and out of your comfort zone. You may be at a point you can relate to Simon Peter when he was challenged by Jesus to launch out. As I made my observations about markers of growth, creating movement, and the current reality in churches, you may have become concerned about a path forward. Conversely, you may believe you are in a good situation. Regardless of how you feel, I want to encourage you to do the following:

1. Do an observational analysis of your Strengths, Weaknesses, Opportunities, and Threats (SWOT analysis).

2. Discern one or two areas of improvement for the coming year and Start Small, Doing it Right to Build it Strong.

3. Strengthen Prayer ministry in the church and each group. Focus prayers on those in your community who are outside of the Kingdom and not connected to a local church.

4. Set a date for launching at least one new group and prepare for the launch. Do not split an existing class, rather seek willing missionaries from current groups to start a group to connect new people to Christ, Community, and Commission.

SECTION 2

GROUPS THAT MULTIPLY

CHAPTER 7

WALKING THE PATH TOGETHER

HONOR ONE ANOTHER ROMANS 12:10 NIV

Whew! As I reflected on the current state of the church, you may be glad that is over and hope I am going to offer you relief. I feel the pain of sharing those stories because each one could have been said of churches I served. Truthfully and maybe surprisingly, each story was from a church considered to be healthy and growing. If we do not stay focused, we will discover our healthy church is growing rapidly toward stagnation and steady decline. Stay vigilant!

We are in this together. Though sarcasm and not encouragement is my gift, I am going to do my best to respect you and the work God is doing through you. My friend Eric Taylor said, "I thought you were going to tell me that everything I was doing was wrong, but instead you gave me tools to analyze and strengthen the work." I appreciated that comment and hope that every reader knows that I have respect for you. You know your local context; I do not. God can guide you as He has guided me. Eileen Mitchell said of me, "Daniel has a thousand ideas. Thankfully, we do not have to do all of them." I love to brainstorm ideas, but you do not have to do any of them. Do the one that God gives you. Always expect to hear from God as you process through these ideas to discover what is best for you and your church. (For the record, Eileen had a thousand good questions, which made her a good ministry partner).

Several years ago, I was asked to assist a church in strengthening its work. I spoke with the pastor who revealed that they had recently had other consultants come to the church. I recognized their names and regarded them as some of the best in the field. I inquired if he would be willing to share with me the results of their work. He agreed and mailed me a copy of the lengthy document. The document was divided into two parts. The first part focused on everything that was unhealthy in the church. The second part was everything that needed to be done to restore the church to full strength and vibrancy.

I read the first part and was distraught. Most of what was said about that church could be said of my church. I quickly moved to part two of the document and became overwhelmed. There was so much to do, and I was too depressed to start. I called the pastor and shared my feelings. He responded by telling me that is how he felt. The church was overwhelmed and had not attempted to get started. I assured him of a few things. First, I am not smart enough nor do I have the desire to do such an exhaustive evaluation. Secondly, if I were invited to come to his church, I would leave them with a single sheet of paper with no more than five bullet points on it. Three of the bullet points would be things they are doing that will make a difference going forward, so keep up the good work. The final two points would be things they could do in the next year that would strengthen the church and give them momentum toward the future.

The church began to thrive in the coming years because they knew where to start small, do it right, and build it strong. In the remainder of this book, I am going to share multiple ideas of what I know will strengthen any church. Do not become overwhelmed but pick a place to start. One or two small things done well this next year will create momentum for a bright future.

To assist you going forward, I am going to share some evaluation tools I use when analyzing a church in terms of mission, vision, and values. The tool is a basic and generic definition that I overlay on the statements made by the church for analytic purposes. It is not detailed, but a quick guide tool.

It is important to know your *why* and as Simon Sinek said *Start with Why.* When you know *why,* your *what* and *how* will become difference makers. Many church leaders tend to adopt the mission, vision, disciples' path, etc. from someone else. We like to get someone's program and run it in our church. I encourage you to do the work of hearing from God and to work with the leaders in developing these statements and descriptions for your church.

Every church should have a mission and vision statement. These statements will answer the question *why*. Certainly, these will be built around the Great Commandment and Great Commission. How you express these passages in your statements will need to be done within the context of your mission field. A simple grid is Love God, Love People, Make Disciples.

Every church should define a disciple. My friend Craig Etheredge describes a 3D disciple: "a disciple is devoted to Jesus, develops the character and competencies of Jesus, and deploys to make disciples who makes disciples." A simple evaluation tool is a disciple abides in and obeys Jesus.

Every church should design a group strategy that will aid in making disciples. A church needs groups that will focus on connecting people to Christ, Community, and the Commission. It is likely that you will need diverse types of groups to accomplish this purpose. Each group needs to know its purpose (*why*), or they will default to being a group focused on biblical content rather than life transformation.

I make distinctions between discipleship, disciple-making, and making disciple-makers. Discipleship is learning core convictions (information). Disciple-making is guiding others to obey (imitation). Both discipleship and disciple-making are needed for a person to become a disciple who abides and obeys the word. The last section of this book will examine how pastors can launch a movement of making disciple-makers.

Every church should develop a disciple pathway. This path will serve as a framework for how the church will accomplish its mission/vision and utilize various ministries to grow disciples. I got to know my friend, Mark Gainey, through his doctoral research on developing a disciple's path. His church's website is designed around the path (myffbc.com). Mark wrote *4 Invitations* to express a simple model for designing a disciple's path. I have used these Invitations through the years as a template for evaluating the path designed by churches. I shared with Mark and Andy Frazier that I believed every path should respond to invitations seen in Scripture: Come and See, Be with Me, Follow Me, and Abide in Me. I will use this path in the next few chapters to suggest how we might strengthen the work of groups in making disciples.

I will introduce **eye-opening moments** on occasion to underscore personal turning points in my understanding. Here is the first **eye-opening moment**. A disciple path is often viewed as how the church will encourage and equip someone to become a follower of Christ. To become a follower of Christ is the starting point and not the destination. The journey is to live and extend the invitations by creating gatherings and groups so that you can guide others to abide and obey by making disciples until He comes again. I observed this in the life of Jesus, and I desire to imitate Him. Therefore, the church must model the path to empower followers to continue the journey wherever God sends them.

At the end of each invitation, you will be given a suggestion or two of how to start small, do it right, and build it strong. However, given the local context, you may decide there is a better place to start. You will continue to be asked to process through the big idea revealed in the chapter, to present a bright idea that struck you as you read, and to pinpoint the better idea for your church with a specific course of action.

YOUR OBSERVATIONS

1. As you have read, what is your Big Idea from this chapter?

2. What is the Bright Idea that has you thinking?

3. What is the Better Idea that you will implement?

CHAPTER 8

DISCIPLE PATHWAY INVITATION #1: COME AND SEE

JOHN 1 NIV

A disciple pathway is presented often in a linear form. It is understandable since we tend to think linearly rather than cyclically. When you are teaching others, invariably you will draw the path and mark stages, steps, phases, etc. A linear diagram gives the mistaken impression that you not only exit a stage, but you also leave it behind. However, you do not leave a phase behind; it becomes a part of your identity. Your identity in Christ is not a noun, but a verb. You are not a disciple, you disciple. We want to express evangelism and discipleship as different wings of an airplane. Wings are wings, and an airplane is grounded without them. Instead of presenting evangelism and discipleship as separate and distinct nouns, present them as a verb: disciple or make disciples.

A better expression of the path is a wheel that indicates motion. Disciple-making is a movement that continues until Jesus returns. The path does not have a finish line, but a line of continuation in the unfinished work of the Great Commission. If you have designed a path, I am not asking you to discard your work but to think about adding the idea of continual movement as opposed to a finish line.

Jesus extends the invitation to come to Him numerous times in Scripture. It is always an invitation to experience the reality that He is the Messiah. To know that He is the source of life, you must come to Him. There is no substitute for a personal knowledge of Jesus. Jesus invited disciples to come to Him, and the disciples invited others to come and see for themselves. There is no greater invitation than to come and see Jesus.

Come and see should be the invitational focus of any gathering. The most obvious gathering is the Church in Worship. Though we want the preaching to be powerful, the music to be inspiring, and the childcare to be topnotch, most of all we desire people to come and see Jesus. Everything should point to Him so that all can discover that He is the Messiah. I will not critique what is happening in gatherings across the globe. I will ask you to evaluate your worship gathering with this question: would a skeptic like Nathanael (John 1:46), leave this gathering knowing that Jesus is the Son of God?

My greater concern in this invitation is the frequency in which it is extended. How many gatherings are you offering where people are invited to come and see? There are obvious additional gatherings like Vacation Bible School, Men/Women's events, seasonal events, and specialty events (car shows, wild game suppers, etc.). You should evaluate each with the Nathaneal question.

Return in your thoughts (or Bibles) to Luke 5. Jesus calls fishers to follow and fish for people. He gives everyone proof that He is the Messiah, and then He calls Levi/Matthew to follow Him. Please note what Levi did, He created a gathering where His friends could come and see that Jesus is the Messiah.

Are groups in your church creating gatherings where the unchurched can explore the claims of Christ? I am seeing the rise of community gatherings where friends are invited to have fun and to hear the testimony of the host or others in attendance. My friends, Gary and Julie Cornelius, called their gatherings Dinner for Eight. This is a good way to partner with another couple from your group to invite two unchurched couples to a come and see Jesus in you. Terri and I have seen good things happen because of these types of gatherings. Ever noticed that the Bible mentions eating often (Acts 2:46)? Friendships are forged over food, and the Lord can be praised in these gatherings.

I had a pastor call and say, "I hate the Spring!" I thought he might have severe allergies, so I began to inquire about his statement. He explained that springtime destroyed visitation. I was confused, so I asked for more information. He told me that baseball is king in the Spring, so people are not home when he goes to visit. My sarcastic nature began to get the best of me, so as politely as possible, I asked, "Where are the people?" "At the ballpark," he exclaimed! I replied, (sarcasm alert) "If you know they are at the ballpark, why go knock on their door?" I could not fault him; I have done it too. I have gone by countless people to knock on the door where no one is home. Instead of going back to where I saw the people, I would go home.

A week later, the pastor called to tell me about the best night of visiting he had ever experienced. He had a church member that helped organize things at the ballpark. He stood in one spot while the church member introduced him to thirty-five people who needed a church home. Within a week, he led a group to launch a ministry to assist parents at the baseball field. He called to report the good news of what was happening and said, "It seems the community is interested in the church that is interested in the community." Every community has centers of wholesome family activity where Sunday School groups could go and serve. Allow the community to create gatherings where others can come and see Jesus in your people. Go where the people are already gathering.

I sat beside a pastor at a ballpark one day and listened as he bemoaned the fact that he could not get young men in his church. As he explained, I looked on softball fields and bleachers full of young men. I asked if he had ever thought about asking his young adult groups to come and serve young men and families to earn the right to invite them to come and see?

It has been said that the key to a growing church is location, location, location. This has never been true. You are His dwelling place: the key is visibility, visibility, visibility. Can others see Jesus in you?

Are you equipping your groups to see the mission field that is all around them? Do they know how to represent Christ wherever they go? My friend Robert Mullins says, "Leverage everything." Wherever you go, whatever you do, seize the opportunity to introduce people to Jesus. Robert uses his skill in art and love of music as avenues into the lives of people who need to know Jesus. My brother, David, serves the local high school as a volunteer sports information director. He has discovered a good way for him to be present and represent Christ in one of largest gatherings in the community. I use Acts 1:8 Prayer cards (See Appendix) to help members discover their mission field.

Survey group members to discover their talents, skills, and abilities. Help them use those for the Kingdom. In one church I served, we had the local sports heroes. I asked them to conduct a sports camp, which resulted in reaching new families for the church. One of the team members said, "Thank you for allowing me to do what I know how to do for the Kingdom." Another church taught music to children in the surrounding area. Shortly, they found themselves starting Bible study groups for the mothers and later, the fathers. This church grew from an attendance of twelve to a hundred twenty in a year with eighty baptisms. Do you lack children? Create gatherings like VBS, sports camps, music camps and anything else that is possible through the skills and abilities of the people in your church.

My wife, children, and I have used numerous means to minister in our community and have seen many come to know Christ as a result. One of the primary ministries is called the brownie ministry. We go to a home and bless the people with a plate of brownies. It is amazing to see the results of simple acts of kindness. We have mowed lawns, cooked meals, and attended gatherings at the homes of neighbors so that they might see Jesus.

It has been a joy to hear the testimony of group members who learned from our example how to be on mission whenever they gather with others. My favorite story comes from one friend who moved his grill to his front yard. He said it always creates a gathering, so cook extra. Your church may have a handful of gatherings in a week, but the community, schools, stores, and workplaces have more opportunities for people to come and see Jesus in you.

Many times, we will not have to create the gathering or try to schedule the perfect time. We need only to lift our eyes and see the harvest field that is before us (John 4). As you have been reading this chapter, how many gatherings are going on in your community where you already have disciples that could be extending the invitation to come and see Jesus? Go where the people are and let them see Jesus in you.

We need to equip people to be on mission in the mission field that God gave them. We tend to bring them off the mission field rather than to equip them for it. Where do your people invest their lives during the week? Disciple them to be disciples wherever they go.

Eye-opening moment: My family visited a crowded worship service where the pastor said, "There is not a person here today that could not reach someone for Jesus this next week." I was stunned. Did this mean the audience was comprised of only believers? Were non-believers absent? How did he know I was a believer? My son was ten years old and quoted the pastor at our lunch table. He said, "Did the pastor mean that?" Though I had trouble with the statement, I assured my son that it was delivered with sincerity. He replied, "Daddy, if everyone invites someone where will those people sit?" We pray and plead, but we do not expectantly prepare.

It is amazing how we preclude the people who need Jesus from our gatherings. We had a gathering where more than twenty people came to know Christ. As you might imagine, I got questioned as to what I did, who spoke, etc. The most important thing was we made sure non-believers were present. We believe in the power of the Word, so we should bring people who need to see Jesus to our gatherings.

Start small: Ask a group to discover or create one gathering outside of the church where they can make Christ known.

Do it right: Let people experience the love of Christ through the actions of the group.

Build it strong: Use that group as a model and mentor for others to be at work on their mission field. Share ideas and insights to encourage one another.

YOUR OBSERVATIONS

1. As you have read, what is your Big Idea from this chapter?

2. What is the Bright Idea that has you thinking?

3. What is the Better Idea that you will implement?

4. For more ideas on any of the 4 Invitations, please read the book *4 Invitations* by Mark C. Gainey.

CHAPTER 9

INVITATION #2: BE WITH ME

MARK 3:13-15 NIV

Mark Gainey, Andy Frazier, and I discussed the four invitations revealing our favorite of the four. As you read my story of beginnings earlier, you may have noticed that I was impacted through a group's strategy. Therefore, Be with Me is clearly my favorite. It is the lynchpin of the invitations. With this invitation, Jesus impacted gatherings and groups, and He revealed how to be a guide who makes disciple-makers. Sunday School, Life Group, Connect Group, or whatever you call it in your church is a passion of mine. As such, this chapter will contain several opportunities for you to process your observations.

What is the difference between a group and a gathering? I use the imagery of Luke 5 where numerous people <u>gathered</u> on the shore to explore the claims of Jesus. The <u>group</u> is found in the boat with Jesus being encouraged toward life change by being sent into the deep. The group was being built toward a mission-focused community. Bible study fellowship is the current descriptor of our groups. Jesus modeled a distinctive style of group, relational and missional, focusing on people growing together to go to the nations.

Some have said, if you can give the church only one hour, then go to our Group ministry. While I understand the sentiment, there is something terribly wrong with someone who knows and loves Jesus affording His bride only one hour per week. My conviction is that gatherings and groups work together to help people come to Jesus. Furthermore, in this day and time, we would be wise to help people encounter Jesus outside the church before expecting them to come inside the church. Remember, the invitation is to come and see Jesus, not come and attend our church (though I want both). What groups can do that gatherings cannot (effectively) is connect people to a witnessing community where than can come to know Christ, grow in His Word, and go to the nations.

Groups must connect people to Christ, Community, and the Commission. Why? Because Jesus started His group for that purpose. This is the image given to us by Jesus in Mark 3. The big picture is that Jesus started small, with a group. Why should you be in a group? Jesus modeled the importance of being in a group. Why should you start groups? Jesus started a new group and continually modeled the importance of groups (feeding the 5,000).

Jesus also did it right. Look at his formula for an effective group in Mark 3. He called those He wanted to be with Him, so he could send them. We will look at these three keys, explore them, and then make some applications that will move us toward an effective group strategy. His focus on reaching, guiding, and sending must be replicated in our churches.

Those He wanted

Most of our groups exist to teach people the Bible. Do you recognize teaching as being a secondary task of a group? Historically, the primary task of Sunday School was to reach people for Christ. Of greater importance, Jesus started His group by reaching out to those He wanted. Who were they? The brightest and best? No, they were ones the Father gave Him as He prayed. Furthermore, Jesus called them from the masses to guide them to reach (fish for people) the nations.

Do your groups have a list of unreached people for whom they are praying and pursuing? Are they actively bringing people to Jesus? Do they share a testimony and a plan of salvation regularly when they meet? If not, why not? My suspicion is threefold: 1) they believe their primary task is teaching a lesson, 2) their fellowship has grown tight (exclusive), and 3) their Bible study is beyond the understanding of a non-believer or new believer.

Through the years, some of my groups have placed a Most Wanted Poster in their room. It is a list of people they want in their group, and they want to know Christ. They include the title, *Most Wanted*, on the poster. If people on the list come to the group, members can explain to them how they are one of the people most wanted in the group. I have heard stories where the new person asks to add a name to the poster.

Posted on the wall or not, each group should have a list of names. Each person in the group should be praying and seeking ways to share or care for the people listed. Notice that Jesus ministered in Simon Peter's home before asking him to be in the group. Jesus and Peter had numerous interactions before the group was formed.

To be with Him

It is not unusual to hear someone told they need to go to Sunday School or get in a group if they really want to get connected to the church. I jokingly say that most people are in Sunday School out of a sense of *oughtness*; you ought to go to Sunday School! Hebrews 10:25 is the rationale for going, "not forsaking the assembly of ourselves together." This is a poor application of Scripture and misses the point of assembling: holding fast to what we know to be true and encouraging one another to love and honorable deeds.

Years ago, it was common for Sunday School and Worship attendance to be equal. Today, both are in decline, and Sunday School is significantly lower than worship attendance. Time could be spent on an analysis of the cause, but I want to focus on a cure.

I love college football. I do have a favorite team, but I like the brand better than other sports. I do not give time to other sports, preferring college football. In late August, stadiums will be full of screaming fans. It is quite a spectacle, which portrays a deep passion for that sport. I have been to some of those stadiums. Though not as rabid as some fans, I still enjoyed the game. What I did not enjoy was the experience of getting there and waiting for necessities. Traffic is horrible. Hunting for a parking space is miserable. The long walk to the stadium is agonizing. The heat (or cold) is unbearable. Standing in line is insufferable. The unreasonable prices are painful to the budget. However, stadiums are still at capacity.

The best seat for college football is in my home, in front of my television. Some people have decided that worship is best in their home, in front of their television. It is likely that I will not go to another game and others will not go back to church. Only one thing will get us to return to either venue: someone who cares asks us to be with them.

Jesus asked those He wanted to be with Him. They did not have to qualify, stand in line, or buy their own ticket. The barriers were non-existent, respond to the invitation and be with Him. The best invitation is to be with Jesus, and we can extend that invitation to others. Just like the men carrying the paraplegic, we should not let anything stand in the way of bringing people to Jesus. Many people began attending church and/or Sunday School at the invitation of a friend or family member. It is still true that people are more likely to attend church at the invitation of a friend. One of the children in the neighborhood that frequents our home, invited us to go to church with him on Easter. He had not learned that I was a pastor; he just knew that he wanted us to be with him. Terri and I talked about if we were not already involved that we would have gone. In ministering in our neighborhood through the years, we have discovered the positive response to the invitation had little to do with our church. Those invited knew nothing about it; they responded to the invitation to be with us. I remember one person saying, "I don't know what Terri Edmonds has, but I want to be like her." Again, visibility is the key. Do people see Jesus in you?

A Tribute

I became a State Missionary in June of 1996. In January of that year, my mom and dad hosted their annual New Year's family gathering. I saw my cousin Keith entering the door. His body once strong was riddled with pain from cancer. I got out of my comfortable chair so that he could sit in it. Realizing this could be our last meeting, I put aside my introverted nature to start a conversation. What transpired is a conversation I will never forget. I discovered something I never knew about Keith; he had become a Sunday School teacher at his local Baptist church. He told me how it happened. He watched for months as parents would drop their children off at church and then go home, shopping, or somewhere other than church. It became an anger issue for him.

In his quiet time, God began to make him look on the people with compassion and see them as He did. These people were not Christians and had little background in church. Therefore, they would not feel comfortable in an existing class; everything would be beyond their understanding. It is likely they would feel ostracized and out of place. He, along with another class member, launched a group for these people. He would reach out to them and ask for their help to become a good teacher. He defined a good teacher as one who could explain everything in a way that everyone could understand. He asked if they would be willing to come and question everything that he said.

He told me that he used LifeWay (Baptist Sunday School Board) curriculum. However, it was merely a tool, a jumping off point for teaching people the Bible. Anytime he used a name, a word, or phrase without proper explanation, someone would make him explain it (even if they knew the answer). He gave me the example of Passover and how you must explain it from Exodus to Jesus in his group.

One thing that resulted from this method of teaching is that he rarely "got through the lesson." With that revelation Keith said, "Now Daniel, you are the Sunday School guy, and you may tell me that I am doing it wrong, but I will keep doing it anyway [I knew him, so I knew that was a fact]. People are coming to know Christ as a result, three last Sunday." Thrilled I said, "Keith, you are doing it right!"

Keith further expressed that he studied the Bible extensively but rarely shared all the knowledge gained with the group. He questioned himself on why he studied so much, then he realized disciples must learn to feed themselves so that you can feed His sheep.

Did Keith have a seminary degree? Was Keith on staff at his local church? The answer to these questions and others like them is no: Keith was a truck driver for United Parcel Service. What Keith had was a burden for a group of people, and he invited them to be with him.

I did get to see him again, but he was already in a coma and would die within the day. I took his hand and prayed a prayer of thanksgiving to God for allowing me to know someone who did it right. A month after his passing, I became a State Missionary. My prayer then and today is to see more people using their group to reach those He wants, to be with Him, so He can send them.

When Jesus invited the disciples to be with Him, He was not an unknown person to them. They had heard Him and seen Him in action. They had been recipients of an aspect of His teaching or ministry. The disciples did not have a deep and abiding relationship with Him, but they experienced His powerful, persuasive words and deeds. The opportunity to be with Him was all the motivation they needed. You do not need games, gimmicks, or great ideas. Jesus in you is still sufficient. I am convinced that when others see Jesus in you, He will draw the people so that they will be with you.

So He could send them

You have heard the phrase, start with the end in mind. Jesus started small, with a group. He did it right as they were with Him. Then he built it strong by sending them fully trained to the nations. If He had kept them, they would have become dependent and lethargic. He sent them while He was still on the journey with them (Luke 9). He received their report (Mark 6) and immediately challenged them to greater things. My friend, Cody Hale, refers to this as resistance training. Jesus would help the disciples develop spiritual strength and stamina through bringing them in and sending them out.

In *Field of Dreams,* you hear whispered, "If you build it, he will come." It is misquoted as "…they will come." The idea of the misquote is an attractional model: see the need, create the solution, and people will come. This is foreign to the teaching of Jesus. He did not build a building so that people would come; He built people so that they would go. You were not built to be present; you were built to disciple the nations. The church is not a place to come to: it is a people who are sent to proclaim the Kingdom.

In John 16 - 18, Jesus says He sends the disciples in the same way the Father sent Him. He was sent to seek and save, to testify to the Truth, to abide and obey by making disciples who will disciple until He comes again. We are not sent to create informational depth, but generational depth as well. Do not disciple your group to a depth of knowledge without sending them to the depths of humanity. Width and depth of are equal importance. Arguably, you cannot get deep in knowledge until you get wide with the Gospel. The wider you go, the more you will seek depth of understanding. The more I share my faith, the more I seek to know Him and the full counsel of His Word. Get off the shore and out of the shallows. Sent to the deep, you will recognize Who you serve.

Jesus started small with one group. He did it right through a relational, missional model. He built it strong by sending disciples to make disciples. I will wrap this with a line I borrowed from Ken Adams: "Jesus started the church the way He wanted it; now He wants the church the way He started it." Ken does not know where the saying originated, but I am certain Jesus did it and the quote is worth saying over and over.

YOUR OBSERVATIONS

1. As you have read, what is your Big Idea from this chapter?

2. What is the Bright Idea that has you thinking?

3. What is the Better Idea that you will implement?

CHAPTER 10

CONTINUATION OF INVITATION #2: BE WITH ME

MARK 3:13-15 NIV

JESUS' MODEL FOR GROUPS: KNOW THEM BY NAME

Values are visible, vocal, and verifiable. If we value bringing people to Christ, if we value building

Community, if we value Commissioning disciples to serve, then we should have their names before us

and talk about ways to Connect them to Christ, Community, or Commission. When Jesus called the

apostles out from the crowd, He knew their names and had sought the Father for them. Jesus began to

guide them toward becoming fishers of people: disciples who make disciples.

A frequent question I receive pertains to meetings with teachers. How often do you have them and what

do you do in the meeting? My response is usually in the form of a question. If the Apostle Paul oversaw

the meeting, what would be discussed? What if Jesus were in charge? One thing is for certain, the

conversation would focus on people: reaching them, equipping them, and sending them out. The

meeting will evaluate the progress that is being made and reveal the next steps involved in making

disciples. How often should you meet? At least monthly in person plus continual contacts to encourage

and equip.

The importance of the meeting increases when we focus on people and moving them toward Christlikeness. Multiple people from each group should be present. One person cannot be responsible for all the work. In times past, it was suggested that a group should have a 1 to 5 ratio of workers to members. This is still a good rule of thumb. As the group grows, grow more people into areas of responsibility.

As Jesus called them by name, they called others. The standout example in connecting people to Christ was Matthew who threw a party. In meeting with group leaders, I challenged them to have multiple fellowships (gatherings) annually. As I challenged them to a dozen or more events, I would hear the concern that it was difficult to do one at Christmas. It is hard to get a single time when every group member can attend any event. The solution is to focus on getting only a few together for a specific purpose at a time. For example, plan an event with a fellow group member to get one or more of your Most Wanted to attend. Two people could invite two others to join them for golf, fishing, a meal, a concert, etc. The purpose may be to share Christ or to connect them to the group. I have created a fellowship to challenge people to be sent out to start a new group. Multiple events like these can take place on the same day.

A highlight for me was to hear the reports of people being connected to Christ, Community, or Commission from those involved. I would hear wonderful stories of people being saved (friends and family), other people would become a part of a group, and new groups would be formed. I enjoyed seeing group members come on Sunday morning with the expectation of seeing one of their Most Wanted people that day. One of my favorites was from a teacher who said, "If I can get them to lunch, I've got them in the group." Again, friendships are forged over food. Much is to be learned from how the

Acts 2 church learned from the model of Jesus.

Jesus' model for groups: Relational

Jesus did not tell them to find a group. He invited them to be with Him. Disciple-making is relational. Acts 1:1 says Jesus began to do and teach. The disciples learned by being with Him. They learned through imitation. The three questions of the disciples in John 14 point to the importance of imitation: how can we know the way, how can we know the Father, and why did you show yourself to us? Jesus responded that He is the Way and others will know the Way through those who are His.

Growing up, if you needed an answer to a question you were encouraged by your parents to look it up. However, if we wanted to know how to do something, we went to a person who could show us how. Reading the steps did not translate as well as watching someone doing each step. Information is best obtained through imitation.

People can go to the internet and get all manner of information. Not all information is reliable or true. The disciples were exposed to all types of information, but Jesus is Truth. I remember singing a song years ago that underscored the reality that actions speak louder than words. You have also heard that more is caught than taught. These idioms point us to why the Bible stresses imitation from Old Testament passages like Deuteronomy 6 to the example of Christ expressed succinctly in Acts 1:1. Likewise, we are to be doers of the Word (James 1).

The goal of groups through the years has been to teach for transformation. Transformation takes place through imitating a life that is being transformed into His image (2 Corinthians 3:18). Remember my Acts 1:1 teacher challenge: what if this Sunday you were allowed to teach only what you do: would your teaching plan change? The truth is that you teach only what you do. Beyond that point you are talking about things you heard. Transformational teaching comes from transforming lives. Can you offer the invitation of Paul: Imitate me as I imitate Christ (1 Corinthians 11:1)?

Jesus model for Groups: Missional

Jesus demonstrated the ultimate purpose of groups, which is to send people. He began with a verifiable value in mind. He did not call the apostles to build a large group but to send them to make more disciples, more groups, and more gatherings. We measure most groups by the number of people in seats as opposed to the number being sent to serve.

The word missional has become a word with a wide array of definitions. I like the definition used by Tod Bolsinger in *Canoeing the Mountains*: a witnessing community. We are indwelt by the Spirit to be witnesses to the ends of the earth, to disciple all nations. As the disciples walked with Him, they became a witnessing community,

Years ago, I wrote an article for Sunday School Leader magazine that was entitled something like, *You Get What You Celebrate.* The premise of the article was that people are motivated toward what is celebrated. If you celebrate perfect attendance, people will strive to be perfect in attendance. Therefore, I began to celebrate the work of disciple-making, which includes sending others. We would commission news groups and celebrate transformation. Jesus' marker of celebration was life transformation. The twelve become disciples that made disciples, the seventy-two, and all were sent into the harvest and returned with joy. As a result, Jesus praised the Father with great joy (Luke 10). Jesus celebrated the disciple-making movement.

Eye-opening moment: As our groups transitioned to a relational-missional model, we were greatly blessed. One group encountered a single mother who needed a place to stay. She had come to know Jesus through the group, and they began to demonstrate the love of a Biblical community. As they helped her find a place, they discovered needed repairs, cleaning, and painting. The group planned a workday, and she invited her friends that did not know Jesus. What a glorious day! The work was done, and her friends were introduced to the Lord. It was an Acts 2 day of celebrating Kingdom additions.

YOUR OBSERVATIONS

1. As you have read, what is your Big Idea from this chapter?

2. What is the Bright Idea that has you thinking?

3. What is the Better Idea that you will implement?

CHAPTER 11

START SMALL, DO IT RIGHT, BUILD IT STRONG GROUPS

MODEL LUKE 5 NIV

"We have some friends that need to be in a group. Listening to you, they will not come unless we start a new group. When can we start?" It is a glorious day when senior adult classes get the vision for connecting friends to Christ, Community, and the Commission. Wonderful things happened in and through those groups in the coming years.

The roadblock to starting new groups is the question, "Where do you get the teacher?" One solution was mentioned in a previous chapter. Every teacher should have an apprentice, and when it is time to start a new group, either teacher can start the new group. However, the struggle continues when you look for an apprentice that is willing to start a new group in the future. One factor in this dilemma is personal doubt by individuals as to whether they will ever be able to teach like the existing teacher. As a State Missionary, I often ask people in the classes I attend if they thought they could be a teacher in the future. Most of them look at the teacher and tell me how they could never teach like him. Some of them respond that way because they are intimidated by the teacher's knowledge, they realize the preparation time that is involved, they are not committed to be in class each week, or they fear someone will ask a question they cannot answer.

I met two couples for lunch and paid for their meal. Everyone knows that if your minister pays for the meal, he is up to something. I began to share with them the names of seven couples not connected to a group. I told them that I was looking for people that could help me reach those people; "Are you the people I'm looking for?" They expressed their interest in reaching out to those people mentioned but said that none of them could teach. I told them I had good news. I do not know what they were thinking, but I am certain they were not expecting this statement; "If none of you have taught, then one of you could not be worse than the other three. Choose from among yourselves because until we reach these people, there is no teaching that will need to be done." One of the men agreed and said, "Let us reach them, and when we get them together, I will try to teach. If I do not improve, then God will raise up somebody else." This was the seedbed for what became a dynamic group that started other groups inside and outside the church.

The previous story represents the common way I started new groups. I would meet with potential group members and talk about people that needed to be in a group. I then would ask if they were willing to help. One of them would assume the role of 'teacher' when the group started, or they knew someone they could ask. I recommend replacing the term teacher with guide since their role is to guide people to study and apply the Bible.

Remember the story from the Exam Time section? The longer a group exists, the deeper the Bible Study level of those in the group. Start new groups to emphasize a relational, missional focus. This is a journey of growing together by studying the Word and applying (obeying) it in daily living.

Develop an expectation that group members will study to get to the HEART of Scripture. To assist in getting everyone to study, develop a mechanism that encourages studying. You might text a few verses to group members each day so they will read the passage during the week.

When you gather, read a few verses, and ask members to share what they **highlighted** and to **express** why that word or phrase caught their attention. Ask members to share questions that came to mind while they read the passage. They may **ask** questions they have or questions they believe the passage resolved. The guides may fear a question being asked they cannot answer. One of the best answers is "I do not know, but we will study that question together before our next meeting." This gives the opportunity for the group to explore the Bible together. Provide trusted online resources group members can use in their study.

Eye-opening moment: I was visiting in a traditional Bible Study class when the teacher posed a question to the group. The person beside me answered, and the teacher said, "Wrong!" I guarantee that type of response will shut off all discussion. I ask people to **express** (HEART) their thoughts or opinions so that they cannot be wrong. I ask guides to explain the Scripture when people ask their questions. This will keep the discussion going while encouraging and equipping people to study the Bible.

Next, involve members in **relating** truth to life. This could involve talking about the commands, promises, examples, actions seen in the passage and how they apply today. Discover the current issues to which the passage applies and how the passage guides us in addressing these issues.

Finally, encourage the group to **tell** someone what they learned or an action they will take because of the study. My friend, Jay Gordon, uses what he calls soft accountability by encouraging the group to pair off or get in triads and share what they will commit to do in the coming week. This subset of the group will pledge to pray for each other during the week. In this subset, each person may also share a prayer need before closing in prayer.

Recently, I modeled this approach for a senior adult group and received positive feedback. They liked the increased participation in the group, not being asked to answer questions, being able to ask questions, and the HEART method of study. One member indicated that she wanted to start a group.

I also use this method with High School students. It raises the level of expectation, participation, and application. Prior to introducing the HEART method, our group time was dominated by my teaching and very little interaction. My daughter, Lydia, observed the group one day and shared that I was intimidating them, and they were afraid to speak and be proven wrong. When we switched roles with them asking the questions, it produced learning readiness and energetic discussions. The questions were exciting, and there were times I would have to say that I needed more time to study before giving an answer.

Does this method lower the bar for the teacher and teaching? No, guides are responsible for studying Scripture, and this should be a regular part of their life. However, they do not prepare to lecture or to ask participants to discuss preset questions. They are to guide the group to seek clear understanding and application of Scripture. They can use case studies to spark discussion, but the focus should be on assisting people in growing in their understanding and application of biblical truth. The goal is not to get through a lesson but to guide people to relate truth to life.

The text for these groups is the Bible. This does not preclude using curriculum, but it is only a tool. It is not uncommon among the groups using the HEART (or similar) method to get behind in dated curriculum. Bible study guides (and I am one) tell me they stay with a passage until they have a sense of mastery in understanding and application. The study nor discussion ends because time ran out for the session. However, sessions do need to have a designated end time.

When it comes to curriculum, LifeWay includes Extras for each study. These can be helpful with icebreaker type questions to get participants ready to dive into the study. For pastors, sermon outlines are often provided if you want to reinforce group studies from the pulpit. An additional feature is the daily discipleship guide for small groups outside of the Sunday School hour. Marc Hodges is having great experiences with his groups using curriculum. Members study in advance and come prepared to share what they have learned and engage in discussion. Marc built up to this change in Sunday School by discipling men to study and apply God's Word. These men would each then disciple some other men. The net impact of that movement on Sunday School and other ministries is clear and powerful. The burden of the class time is not on one person. Occasionally, he preaches on the same passages and d-groups utilize the same passages for further understanding and accountability. What a wonderful way to start small, do it right, and build it strong.

Several pastors prefer sermon-based groups. This means the pastor becomes the teacher through the Sunday morning sermons. The objective is the same for the group with each member expected to have read and reflected on the Scripture and sermon before coming to the group meeting. Robert Mullins and I used a sermon-based model to start new groups.

When I sat down with Robert, he said they needed new groups especially for Young Adults. The problem he said was "They lacked bench strength." This was his way of describing their lack of teachers. For seven weeks, we invited all guests to come to a large group with the pastor as the teacher. The first week, it was reported that forty percent of those in attendance did not usually attend LifeGroup. Three existing groups were brought to the Fellowship Hall along with the guests. Roundtables were used to form groups. Each table had a host who had the responsibility of inviting people in their age group to seat at their table. When questions were given, the host would make sure everyone had the opportunity to talk or ask a question of the pastor. A new model of studying together was introduced, and by the end of the seven weeks, multiple new groups formed. When table hosts discovered their responsibility was not lecturing but engaging people in the study, they were ready to start a group.

The main objective of the HEART method is spiritual movement. It is a way to grow people through the milk, meat, model, and mission stages so that multiplication will take place. In a nutshell, these are the stages seen in Luke 5 as Jesus moved people from the shore to the shallows, to be sent into the deep, to be set apart for a great mission.

Caution: there is a difference between starting a group and splitting a group. Anytime people are forced to leave their existing group, you have split a group. This will produce a negative attitude toward starting new groups. Always seek volunteers to start new groups, even if they are short-term missionaries with a plan to return to their existing group after six months or a year. Notice that Jesus did not force the disciples to follow, but He invited them to a greater mission.

Other considerations: Missional

Soft accountability to tell someone what you have learned is the starting point in becoming a missional community. You are introducing the idea of sharing what Jesus is teaching you. Open each session with an opportunity for someone to share a positive result or occurrence from the previous study. I usually give members an opportunity to share something good that happened this week. My hope is that when people are studying the Word and spending time in prayer, they will learn to share what God is doing in their life.

You will want to teach the group members how to share their testimony and a plan of salvation. Each week, give members the opportunity to share their testimony and allow someone to share the plan of salvation (even if notes are needed). This will help them get comfortable with this as being a normal aspect of Christian living. Plus, everyone gets to hear the plan of salvation every week. It is getting more challenging to get people to come at a separate time to learn and practice soul winning (though it is worth it). This may be a better time to equip people to share with those on their most wanted list.

More Abundant Life by Lawrence Phipps is still my favorite new believer material. The book is designed to be used one on one in immediate disciple-making. However, after it was written, Lawrence and I used it in every group so that group members would review the basics of their faith and learn how to disciple a new believer. It is complete with verses to memorize and other exercises that are beneficial to group health. *More Abundant Life* or something similar (*First Letters* by Larry Hyche) is a necessary tool for creating a missional or witnessing community.

Other ideas to strengthen the group: Responsibilities

Years ago, my brother's church had to have some groups meet at a nearby school until they could build additional space. The day came when everyone could meet on campus, but after the first few weeks, attendance began to drop dramatically. He called and asked me what I thought was happening. My response was to tell him that he was suffering from unemployment. When the groups were meeting at the school, numerous people had to come early to set up, help people park, greet people, and numerous other tasks. When they came back to campus, those jobs went away. Without a responsibility, Sunday

School becomes optional. Over the next few weeks, he began to give people new responsibilities, and attendance steadily increased.

Arthur Flake, in *True Functions of the Sunday School,* said Sunday School needed to function as the employment agency of the church. His book was written in 1930. Where did he get such an idea? It comes from Luke 5 and other places where Jesus called His disciples to a work, fishing for men. Jesus did not call His disciples to be passive listeners, but active doers of the mission. I believe people today do not need another meeting; they need a worthwhile mission. An effective guide will engage others in the work.

When assisting Lawrence Phipps in writing *Growing Sunday School TEAMS*, we saw the group ministry as a starting point for discovering the work God is calling you to do. It was essential to involve as many people as possible in some aspect of the work so that you could equip them, encourage them, and send them to serve. We are the body of Christ, and each person has a place to serve (1 Corinthians 12).

Other ideas to strengthen the group: Group Time

Jay Gordon has led out in developing a strategy for use during the group time called the 5 Looks. Mark Gainey and I have slightly different versions of this methodology. Jay uses look around (fellowship), look up (prayer), look down (Bible study), look ahead (challenge for the week), and look back (soft accountability and celebration). The first three are self-explanatory but the last two need an explanation. Always challenge group members based on the study and ask them to commit with their accountability partner or in the triad they form. They may discover their own challenge, or you may suggest one. A challenge needs to be specific and verifiable (search smart goals). Prayer with a partner or triad creates soft accountability. The following week, look back on the week by asking members to share any celebrations that resulted from the prior week's study.

Explanation of Terms: Relational versus Relationship

I have used the term relational without definition or distinction from relationship. Relational is an adjective and used as a descriptor of the group methodology. A relationship is a noun that characterizes the dynamic that exists between two or more people. My hope is to express that the group understands that it must be relational in connecting people to Christ, Community, or Commission. The groups do not have to build deep and lasting relationships with anyone outside or inside the group. To be relational means you make a personal connection with those being sought. Deep relationships take more time to develop and tend to prevent the starting of new groups as evidenced by this oft repeated phrase, "I would just miss my friends too much." If new groups are not started within a year to eighteen months, strong relationships will form and resistance will grow.

This is also true when it comes to witnessing. Who are the two hardest groups of people for evangelistic endeavors? People you have never met and people that you know very well. The optimum time for sharing your faith is soon after making a relational connection.

Deep relationships cause us to spend time with our friends and family. This is important, but it is of equal importance to spend time connecting people to Jesus. Leverage your relationships to be relational toward those who need Jesus.

Essentials in starting a new group

1. Prayer.

    a. Pray for wisdom.

    b. Pray for a core team, people who want to reach others.

    c. Pray for people who need to be reached.

2. Personally visit with the core team God has laid on your heart.

    a. Break bread together.

    b. Get to know each other.

    c. Share the names of people not in a group.

    d. Ask if they will help in reaching these people.

3. Pattern the group after Mark 3.

    a. Reach out to people who are wanted for the group.

    b. Remember the invitation is to be with you.

    c. Realize the purpose (*why*) is so that people can be sent.

4. Plan with the core group.

    a. People to be reached.

    b. Place to meet (on campus or off campus).

    c. Practices to be utilized in bringing people into the group.

5. Principles.

    a. Reaching before teaching.

    b. Involvement before instruction.

    c.   Model the mission before multiplication.

6.   Pick a launch date. (Often this is the first thing to do. It creates commitment).

7.   Prepare for the harvest through prayer.

YOUR OBSERVATIONS

1. As you have read, what is your Big Idea from this chapter?

2. What is the Bright Idea that has you thinking?

3. What is the Better Idea that you will implement?

CHAPTER 12

INVITATION #3: FOLLOW ME

MATTHEW 16:24, LUKE 9:23, MARK 8:34, MATTHEW 28:19-20

As I shared the four invitations pathway with pastors, I would be questioned about the order. Some believed that Follow Me (Mark 1) precedes Be with Me (Mark 3). While I understand their argument, Mark 1 is specific to the twelve and is still in the exploration phase for them. In effect, it is still come and see that Jesus is the Messiah. Upon the declaration of the disciples that He is indeed the Messiah, Jesus gives the definition of being a disciple to all who dare to follow. Those who believe He is the Messiah, no longer try to save their lives but lose their lives for Him. When you believe in Him, your identity is in Him (Galatians 2:20). A disciple is who you are, denying self and taking up the cross.

With this invitation (Follow Me), Jesus begins to model the Way of the cross. He shows them how to live boldly, not ashamed of the cross, in the sinful generations to come. Before the inner circle (Peter, James, and John), He is transfigured, and His deity (glory) is revealed. Jesus is the fulfillment of the law and the prophets, so we are to obey (follow) Him. The disciples started following an expert teacher. Now they are followers of the Messiah.

Inside the church, we address Follow Me by helping believers develop Christlike disciplines or competencies. This is accomplished by large groups where a leader shares content and invites the learner to practice what was learned. Another approach to developing competencies is in small groups where accountability for application and action is presented. Mentoring is also utilized to develop competencies.

During my early years, the church used organizations or programs like Training Union, Church Training, or Discipleship Training to develop disciples into church leaders. I remember an early acronym the was used; DEPTH which stood for doctrine, ethics, polity, theology, and history. We were given a role to play or assigned a topic (parts) to prepare for the next session. These approaches still exist in some shape or fashion though they have different names.

Did these approaches help me become more Christlike? A disciple? They certainly gave me the information needed, but very little imitation. I had the content and character knowledge with a measure of accountability. I did develop skills in areas of church ministry, but I cannot say that I could make disciples who would make disciples by imitating Christ. I could be a group leader on numerous topics and demonstrate some skills, but I was not a guide trained to guide others to take up the cross. Thankfully, what was lacking in the classroom setting was covered in mentoring through a "do and teach" model.

Should churches continue to offer these types of approaches to making disciples? Yes, but churches may find it difficult to accomplish in the old format. I do believe it will be difficult to disciple all nations through this approach since curriculum or a companion to scripture is needed to assist in multiplication.

Another factor to consider is the goal of these groups. They are meant to make disciples. However, what is the multiplication point, the measure of success? The original intent was to create leadership for new groups or ministries. We would refer to this as a leadership pipeline today. Sadly, the pipeline began to decline in production, and we struggled for group leaders.

Resources

There is an abundance of resources available for this invitation. I avoid recommendations because each resource can have a different definition of disciple and a different outcome. Some intend for the guide to be multiplied. As an example, if four men are in the huddle/group, then each man is meant to disciple others who will disciple others. Other resources are an aid to multiplying group leaders and groups. In this scenario, everyone in the group will become a disciple but not all are expected to disciple others. The hope is to get an increase in the number of groups involved in discipleship.

Truthfully, it is not the resource but the users that determine the outcome. Left on their own, people will utilize a group strategy as they have in the past. They will attend the group until they have accomplished their goal and then move on to something else, or they will try to make the group an ongoing group: no one leaves!

Likewise, there are resources available for short-term competency development. The pastor or assigned staff will develop a university approach where members can sign up to attend a study that addresses a deficiency in their walk with the Lord. Marriage, family, finances/stewardship, doctrine, and other topics may be addressed in these groups.

What should you do?

The answer to this question is based on your mission, vision, and values. If you are a pastor or teacher, do you know your purpose? Read Ephesians 4:11 carefully. Christ gave you to the church for a specific purpose. I caution my fellow pastors not to read into that verse and think you are God's gift to the church (smile), but you are given to the church to equip. You are in your church to equip the people for the work defined by the mission, vision, and values that God gave you for where He has placed you.

In short, I cannot answer the question for you. I can say that I am a groups guy by passion/training and an equipper by calling. I believe everything I do should be pointed toward disciple-making. I was once asked how I made teachers for all the groups I started. My response was "I don't make teachers. I am not called to make teachers. I am not sure I am a good teacher, but I am called to make disciples from whom God raises up teachers (guides)." I developed five basic disciplines that I wanted to see in every disciple, and then I would help them discover ways that could equip others to be disciples. Multiplication was a preferred outcome though it does not come by my hand, nor is it the end goal. In the following chapters, I will share more on what I believe lies beyond multiplication.

Stop designating leaders; disciple them

As I buckled into my seat on the airplane, the pilot announced a delay due to the lack of a co-pilot. The pilot explained that, hopefully, one would soon be found, and we could be on our way. With this announcement, the lady in the seat next to me said, "Why don't you volunteer to be the co-pilot." I refused pointing out that I am not a pilot, lack a license, and have zero training. The only criterion for her request: I was present.

No one wants to be operated on by an untrained, but available volunteer (I know because Jamie Baldwin and I have volunteered). No corporation wants the person at the helm to be void of training and experience, regardless of the hotel they stayed in the previous night. Yet, in our churches, we will entrust our most precious ones to individuals without experience, training, and (at times) a vibrant relationship with Christ. How does someone get nominated to these key positions? They are frequently present and visible to the nominating committee. My illustration through the years has been this: come once a month, you are active; twice a month, you are regular; three times a month, you are on the radar screen of the nominating committee and will be asked to serve. When the church designates leadership in such a manner, the result can be devastating.

I have been guilty of designating leaders. Frustration and desperation can cause you to do things you should not do. It should have been no surprise that when I designated leaders, they struggled and/or quit. I love people who volunteer, but this is an invitation to help them discover what God wants to do through them (Ephesians 2:10). God's church does not lack servants; it lacks disciples responding to His call. Make disciples who will respond to His call.

Start Small, Do It Right, Build It Strong

If I am going to guide you in this invitation, I must tell you that I did not address this invitation in the local church until I started small in the previous phase. Until we started some healthy Be with Me groups, any other ministry was disjointed. I had a layperson who was the Director for Discipleship Training get very frustrated with me over my conviction. I asked him to trust me that when we got Sunday School groups modeled after Jesus' groups model, then Discipleship Training would be needed by the people in those groups. I told him the problem was not that Discipleship Training had died, but that it relocated to Sunday School.

Within the year, several new Sunday School groups were started (and doing it right), and those groups drove the need for further discipleship. The increases in Sunday School and Discipleship Training numerically matched. The methodology of both organizations matched the path with Sunday School designed to reach (Be with Me) and Discipleship Training to equip (Follow me). We renamed Discipleship Training to Discipleship Life since you were being guided to apply truth to life, to obey all things commanded.

Eye-opening moment: I interviewed those who were now going to Discipleship Life to ask this question: if we had not redesigned both organizations would you be involved in discipleship? The answer was in the negative. Their explanation was that if both organizations continued to be about content, then they were getting all the in-depth Bible study they needed in Sunday School. I am convinced most groups formed in the local church focus on the same things: fellowship, prayer, and in-depth content. Follow Me groups should "do and teach" (Acts 1:1).

I will say the place to start in equipping the church is prayer, and when you have healthy groups, begin equipping disciples in studying the Word, prayer, and sharing their faith. Keep in mind, a Follow Me guide must be active and growing in the discipline they teach. These groups must value imitation over information because more will be caught than taught.

Start Small: Consider Preaching through the Disciplines

Do it Right: Start groups to encourage accountability for the practice of each discipline.

Build it Strong: Encourage those equipped to equip others.

YOUR OBSERVATIONS

1. As you have read, what is your Big Idea from this chapter?

2. What is the Bright Idea that has you thinking?

3. What is the Better Idea that you will implement?

CHAPTER 13

INVITATION #4: ABIDE IN ME JOHN 15

. . . WITHOUT ME YOU CAN DO NOTHING JOHN 15:5 NKJV

I received the most questions on this invitation. Should not the invitation be Multiply? Why not Bear Fruit?

I recognize others have used multiply or bear fruit when developing their pathway. I applaud them for their efforts, but I could not go in that direction. I was a product and promoter of the Church Growth movement. The movement was very principle based and program driven. The principles remain, but programs got hammered by the 1980's. Without much discussion, suffice it to say, the 1980's moved us toward a 24/7 society. Businesses that were closed on Sunday's were open every day. I remember that in school, Wednesday was church night, and no homework was assigned. Coaches had to have you showered and out the door by 5 p.m. This all went away during the 1980's, and it became exceedingly difficult to get people to commit to a programmed approach to making disciples. In fact, attendance frequency declined to one or two Sundays per month for many church members.

By the 1990's, people became increasingly committed to activities that had no eternal significance. However, it was not the external culture that stunted the church. Internally, we fixated on producing results and departed from the identity of the Great Commission. The church was in decline, and the Southern Baptist Convention began a downward spiral. Many leaders stuck to the tried-and-true programs and the principles that brought growth in earlier years.

Despite this trend, I was serving at a church that experienced revival. My pastor, Lawrence Phipps, noted what was happening and asked if I would write down everything I was learning so that it could be shared with others. I tore off a corner from a sheet of paper and wrote three words: prayer, prepare, and prayer. Those three words summarized what I knew: Pray to the Lord of the Harvest for Laborers, prepare for a Harvest, and pray expectantly for a Harvest. I wondered what became of that torn piece of paper. I feared that the opportunity to co-write what God was teaching us had been lost with my quick action that night. Months later I discovered that piece of paper under the glass on the pastor's desk. Those three words still summarize all I know about what needs to happen in His church.

Disciples Abide and Obey

The church did not decline because the principles no longer worked, but because the power resides only in Him. Leaders got so good at following and teaching the principles that they forgot that He is the power source. Fruit that remains (multiplication) comes from abiding in the vine. It has been interesting and refreshing to see numerous leaders coming back to build a fervent prayer strategy. The most important function of the church is prayer (Isaiah 56:7 and Matthew 21:13).

Disciples are driven to prayer out of their love for God. Love is an act of will. In showing His love for the Father, Jesus surrendered His will for the will of the Father. If we abide in the love of Jesus (John 15:9), we will obey the will of the Father (Romans 12). How do we abide in the love of Jesus? Obey, keep His commandments: Love God and love each other (John 15:17). As such, abiding and obeying are inseparable. If you are disobedient, you are not abiding. If you are obeying but not abiding, you are self-glorifying. Working on your own strength leads to failure.

The Great Commission reveals our identity as disciples (having gone) who are abiding in Him until the end of this age. We live out our love and identity by making disciples of all nations; guiding people to abide (baptized in Him) and to obey all things He commanded.

Called by a pastor to assist his leaders, I walked in the room and sat down with some familiar faces of well-respected leaders. One whom I considered to be very gifted in Sunday School spoke and said, "We know we need to start new groups, but we are at the age-old question, where do we get the leaders?" My response left him deflated at first: "There is a reason it is an age-old question. No one has answered it." With that, he looked at the pastor as if to say, why did you bring him here if he cannot help us? I continued, "The Bible never comes to that question. We need to learn to ask the right question. Are we abiding and obeying?"

Eye-opening Moment: Thus far, we have looked at a group's approach to making disciples. Abide in Me represents the smallest and most intimate group: God and you. This group is the foundation for continuation. We observed Jesus through gathering the masses, creating relational-missional groups to be sent, and guiding the few as He began to do and teach. In Mark 6, as they were sent to proclaim the Kingdom, the masses followed them back to Jesus. However, before the gathering, the disciples "reported to Him all they had **done and taught**" (Mark 6:30). Those who abide and obey will be sent to do and teach so that the masses will Come and See Jesus. Thus, the path continues throughout all generations. The smallest group will cause the greatest impact.

Start Small: Personally increase your prayer life.

Do It Right: Guide key leaders to increase their prayer life.

Build It Strong: Lead the church to become a House of Prayer.

YOUR OBSERVATIONS

1. As you read, what is your Big Idea from this chapter?

2. What is the Bright Idea that has you thinking?

3. What is the Better Idea that you will implement?

CHAPTER 14

SECTION CLOSING THOUGHTS

…YOU GIVE THEM SOMETHING TO EAT LUKE 9:13

I love the story of the feeding of the five thousand. It is the only miracle of Jesus found in all four gospels. What stands out in this miracle? Jesus' compassion, love for the masses, and willingness to lead the few to make sure the masses are well-fed. The disciples were engaged in creating groups and distributing the loaves and fish. Our churches need to be reminded of our responsibility to feed the masses the Living Bread. We need to have compassion on the masses, invite them into a group, feed them from the Word, and send them out as witnesses to the ends of the earth.

Please note that Jesus' group, disciples, created the gathering as they were sent from village to village. Groups need to create gatherings. Jesus helped them to see and work on their mission field. As they gathered people into towns and villages to "proclaim the Kingdom," these people followed them to Jesus. My prayer is that our people will proclaim the kingdom wherever they go so that people will follow them to Jesus.

Notice that Jesus' group was designed to reach. They were fully equipped for the mission, not needing to take anything extra. They went where they were welcomed and made Jesus known among the people.

The Jesus design and the historic Baptist design for groups is to reach people, to be a witnessing community.

As I read the story and saw that people were satisfied, I observe this as an indication that they were now prepared to share the Truth about Jesus. Shortly after feeding the five thousand, we observe more disciples being sent into the harvest. Groups can and must make disciples who abide in and obey the Word by guiding others to become disciples of Jesus and disciple-makers who go for Him.

I use a track visual to help me see groups multiplication (See Appendix). Another visual might be a funnel where large masses (gatherings) are moved into smaller groups (groups and guides) until they abide and obey to be sent by God to the nations. Another aspect of the track visual depicts the movement started by Jesus that I hope pastors will start in their churches. It starts with the one who guides a few to abide and obey. The few being guided will influence others to be in groups that are sent to create gatherings where people may come and see Jesus. This may appear visually as an upside-down funnel. Regardless of the visual you use, I want to encourage you toward the following:

1. Pray, Prepare, Pray. Pray to the Lord of the harvest for laborers. Prepare a group strategy for reaching an identified harvest field (See Appendix for Connect:316). Pray for the harvest.

2. Launch one new group designed for reaching. If reaching is not the priority, there will not be new people to teach.

3. Encourage the group toward a relational-missional model that engages people in learning and applying God's Word. Utilize the HEART method and 5 Looks in the group.

4. Start small and learn. Do it Right and focus on those outside the group. Build it strong by sharing what you learn as new groups are formed.

SECTION 3

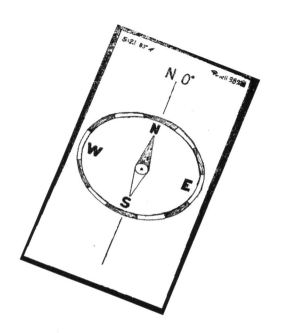

GUIDING A MOVEMENT OF
MULTIPLYING DISCIPLES

CHAPTER 15

4 INVITATIONS IN REVERSE 2 TIMOTHY 2:1-2 NIV

Pastor, you do not have to correct everything you have discovered about your church. You do not have to start at the beginning of the pathway and remove every obstacle in the way. In a Zoom Conference held at the Alabama Baptist State Board of Missions, Bill Hull said, "Don't announce the revolution." Pastor, you do have a calling and opportunity that no one else in your church has; to start a movement of multiplying disciples that will go to the nations starting in Jerusalem.

I still consider Lawrence Phipps to be my pastor. When I gave him a copy of *4 Invitations,* I told him that when he read it, he would recognize some pastors will work the path in reverse. To start a movement of disciples that make disciples, pastors must take up the mantle of walking the path from Abide in Me toward Come and See. We interviewed Bill Hull in the early days of the disciple-making movement. A second chair leader (a person who is not the pastor and has responsibility for discipleship), asked if anyone other than the pastor could start a disciple-making movement in the local church. Bill gave an emphatic no but said everyone should plow the ground they are given.

Second chair leaders must focus on multiplication. They are responsible to bring about organizational change that will create the multiplication of groups that enable people to become devoted followers of

Jesus. I still consider myself a "groups guy," so I understand this tribe's heart and hurts. I understand how some long for their pastor to launch a movement of disciples who make disciples to make disciples.

I also have been a pastor and worked with pastors of all types of churches. I know their hearts and hurts. I know their longing for someone to come alongside to guide the internal processes of the church. Lawrence Phipps and I were this type of team. He would tease me by saying, "It takes a really good Minister of Education to beat not having one at all." I think he still has me in the "really good" category. I am thankful that he led the movement and encouraged me as I developed a multiplying groups model in our churches.

Pastors, you are given to your church to equip its people for the most important work; to make disciples that make disciples of all nations with generational depth until Jesus returns. You are called to more than multiplication; you are called to lead the movement as Jesus modeled it. Pastors can be tempted to settle for multiplication because bodies, budgets, and baptisms are what get counted, evaluated, and noticed most in the church. A disciple-making movement begins small and unnoticed. You will be accused of exclusivity when people notice. The movement begins and moves too slowly for most people. A movement is oven, slow cooker, or smoker compared to the multiplication microwave. Yet, everything from oven, slow cooker, or smoker smells and tastes better; worth the wait.

Does it sound too difficult? **Start Small, Do it Right, Build it Strong!**

. . . competing according to the rules 2 Timothy 2:5 NIV

My parents, Bobby and Maie, were great influences in my life. I do not know if I will ever match my mother's love for Scripture. My forever mental picture of her will be of early mornings seeing her in the

Word and prayer (having a cup of coffee with the Father). My dad is a life-lesson teacher. Everything is connected to a Bible truth. The stories are too numerous and comical to tell, but they will never be forgotten. One of my most frustrating, yet impactful, memories occurred when he would make a last-second rule change to make sure that my brother, David, or I would not beat him. In exasperation, I asked him why he would do that to us. He explained, "In life, you do not always control the rules, but you can control your attitude and actions. You can keep playing to win or quit, which will it be?" He presented 2 Corinthians 4 in a form so that we could understand that the Word applies to every aspect of life.

When the rules change: Do not lose heart, play to win

I listened to my friend Craig Etheredge share his story, but it is a story that many could share. His church in Oklahoma was analyzed by some respected leaders. Their report in summary said, relocate or die. Relocation was not an option for multiple reasons. The rules had changed, and the game looked like it was over. However, Craig and a handful of men decided they were not going to quit. If they were to lose, they would lose staying faithful to the Commission. I came to know Craig through a mutual friend, Rick Howerton, when I asked Rick to identify the number one disciple-making pastor in America. He named Craig as being the best. When the rules change, play to win.

You may be feeling the effects of cultural or church rules changing. Things are not like they used to be. The difficulty of overhauling the church may be making you want to leave and seek greener pastures. You want to, like my dad would say, take your toys and go home. But you are home, right where God placed you for a time such as now. **Start small, do it right, build it strong!**

How small? You and God

See if any of the following sound like your situation?

1. The church is stagnant at best.

2. You feel isolated and alone.

3. Sunday School is filled with "I shall not be moved" classes.

4. You are not a groups guy and making changes in Sunday School is a non-starter.

5. You are bi-vocational, and your hands are full.

6. You do not need one more program to implement.

7. You do not have a mission or vision statement.

8. Everyone does what is "right in their own eyes."

9. The baptistry has not been used in a long time.

10. There is so much to do, you do not know where to start.

If any of these resonate with you or you could expand the list, I have good news. You can be cheerful in trouble because He has overcome (John 16)! Abide and obey. Start small, just God and you. Remember in Him you are not fighting to win; you are fighting from victory to final victory. He has overcome, and you are more than a conqueror through Him (Romans 8:37).

Once you return to the prayer closet and begin to abide and obey, find three others, and teach them how to abide and obey (Follow Me). If you do not think you know how to guide others, you are not alone. You are not the only pastor with that issue. Other pastors have said the same thing.

God burdened my heart to start a disciple-making movement in Alabama. The question I had for Him was, how do I do that? I saw pastors who were trying to create a movement on a national level, but it entailed using their material and developing groups who would multiply. I enjoyed hearing them, and it was inspirational, but not practical for pastors who felt like their plate was already full. You need a pastor(s) who will walk with you on the long journey. If I were going to start a movement in Alabama, I needed to invest in like-minded pastors who would invest in others.

The first pastor I asked to walk with me on this long journey was Robert Mullins. I have known him for thirty years. As God led me to talk with Robert, I knew that he was passionate about making disciples, that he had been discipled, and that he had a strong network of relationships. He is the director of PassionTree Network, which brings together pastors who will focus on making disciples. We worked together for his church. He utilized my group's multiplication knowledge combined with his disciple-making movement model to revitalize the church.

I shared with him my desire, and we prayed through the process of creating a movement. We felt like we needed to create a **gathering** to discover other like-minded pastors. We asked Craig Etheredge to join us for the event. As he shared, we began to discover pastors who wanted to create a movement of multiplying disciples in their church. The next phase was to bring those with interest into a smaller **group** to be with us to send them into the movement. In that group, we discovered pastors who said they wanted to create a movement but have never been discipled like what had been described. Glenn Sandifer, aka Cuz, asked Robert what he would do to help those in that position. Suddenly, we were in the 'follow me" phase providing "huddles" where disciple-making pastors would **guide** others to abide and obey. Hundreds of pastors participated in huddles and began to create a movement of disciple-makers in their church. They started small, by abiding and obeying **God** and leading a small group of men to abide and obey. They started the movement in their church, and God has done a wonderful work in their midst.

Pastor, you can have pastors walk with you in this journey. You may know that you are a disciple, but you have never attempted to create a movement of multiplying disciples. Reach out to me or one of the pastors mentioned in this work, and they will walk (huddle) with you.

Will the movement impact the church wholistically?

Those in the movement you start will impact the whole congregation. Marc Hodges shared how those who have been discipled enable their Sunday School group to focus more on leading people to study and live the Word. These disciples also start groups in the community as well. Mark Gainey, Andy Frazier, Cody Hale, Robert Mullins, and Eric Taylor are pastors that can share similar experiences, plus they are the leaders of the Alabama Disciple Making Movement.

Will I have to change everything and start another program?

Disciple-making is inviting people into your life. Pastors refer to disciple-making as 'doing life together.' Robert, Andy, Mark, and I went to the home of a disciple-making legend, Robert Coleman, aka Clem. We were thrilled to listen and learn. Finally, the obvious question came: "How did you start?" He told a gathering of students that he studied and prayed every morning in his office; anyone could join him. He made no great fanfare about it; he offered a simple invitation. About four students joined him, and the movement was underway. Pastor, can you get three or four to study and apply the Word of God with you? The invitation requires no additional curriculum, no program, no campaign but an invitation to do with you what you already are doing.

What if I want to use a curriculum or resource?

You are the pastor, do as God guides you. I prefer not to use curriculum or a resource that is not available in the language of all nations. If you do, it could limit you or your multiplied guides in the future. I also believe the Bible is sufficient for the mission God has given to us.

If I were to use a curriculum, I would consider the LifeWay curriculum line being used in my church. You will find LifeWay offers discipleship guides to go along with the curriculum. Additionally, you will find they have on-line resources to help you, including sermon outlines. The sermon aids will help you focus the congregation and your disciples on the same passage and practices throughout the week. I applaud LifeWay for going the extra mile in resourcing our churches for disciple-making. I caution that you must study what Jesus did in making disciples so that you understand the difference between a group multiplication model and a disciple making movement to all nations.

I have friends and acquaintances that have written material for making disciples. I know that pastors may prefer to utilize these over the Bible alone. Again, you are the pastor, do as God guides you. I have encouraged the pastors in the Alabama Disciple Making Movement to watch for holes or gaps. Some have discovered the material is not suitable for a new adult believer. Some have noted difficulties with the length of time needed, too short or too long. Other observations include that the material adds one more thing for everyone to study, is not affordable, does not include key disciplines, etc. I will be glad to connect you with people who are using the same resources as you.

One final caution, we are familiar with programs and treat all resources as such. We expect that it has a shelf life or that the church will stop using it. We complete programs and move to something new. When the pastor leaves, the new pastor will start something new. The Bible is the authority for our lives and reveals our identity in Christ: use it.

How and where do I start?

I have given you two starting places; groups multiplication or pastor-led movement. If you are the pastor, I recommend a both/and strategy. Seek to start one group with its focus on reaching new people. I have included numerous ideas and suggestions for starting the group. You will want this group to be the model of future groups, so use the reproducible model of Jesus found in the Be with Me invitation. I would then start the movement the way Jesus did. Through prayer, allow God to lead you to the three or four men that He wants in the movement. You may use the gathering to groups to guides model mentioned in starting the movement in Alabama. While you are praying for the people He wants, begin preaching (gatherings) on disciple-making and why He wants us to fish for people. Select existing groups to share what it means to be a disciple and disciple-maker. These groups might include elders, deacons, or your staff. As you preach and share, be listening to God and His people. He will help you see those He wants as guides in the movement. Remember, Peter, James, and John were in gatherings and a group before being called to a closer relationship as guides of the future disciple-making church.

How do I involve both men and women in the movement?

It is not appropriate for a man to disciple women and vice versa, so this is a frequently asked question. I will offer two answers. First, if you have a staff that includes women, then start the movement with your staff. Secondly, you may start the movement with couples and move to men with men and women with women in the second generation.

What do I do in a typical meeting?

I asked Mark Gainey to write the non-curriculum curriculum. Strange name, I know, but Mark accomplished the task in his book, *Disciple Making Toolbox*. In the book, Mark answers this question and many others like it. He also provides you with access to a website so that you can put together your customized toolbox. I will not leave you with that (shameless) promotion. I believe your time should include a relationship building time. I usually ask my disciples to share the best thing that happened and their biggest prayer need. We will have a time of prayer. I usually include a Scripture memory or other challenge for the week, and there is a time of accountability after our prayer. Since I like to use the Bible as the sole resource, we will have a time to share our HEART with one another. I will focus on the R and T by way of challenge for the coming week. I do want those in my group to begin seeing the mission field that God has for them at home, work, community, and activities. Conclude the time with prayer. One caution, there is more to making disciples than a weekly meeting. You need to take them on adventures where you "do and teach." Eventually, they will need to lead out in these activities before guiding others to become disciple-makers.

How long do I disciple them?

You can get a variety of answers to this question. The answer for me is that I send them once I know they are abiding and obeying so that they are doing and teaching. I want them living as a disciple wherever they go. When they come to you reporting those things they have done and taught (Mark 6:30), then they are in the final stages of readiness.

What if I need help?

I am willing to help anyone; however, if you are an Alabama Baptist, I am your missionary. I am not the only Alabama Baptist State Missionary that is willing to help you. Reach out to one that you know for the assistance you need.

Also, I would be remiss in failing to mention that you have an Association Mission Strategist that will resource and help you. Learn to network with pastors and leaders in your association to advance the Kingdom.

If you live outside Alabama, our Disciple Making Ministries team will help you. However, you also have some capable State Missionaries that will be glad to assist you.

Start small, Do it Right, Build it Strong!

A friend told me about being in a heated discussion over disciple-making terminology. He identified Bill Hull as the person who stood and said we are using the same words but with different definitions. The goal of everyone was to make disciples.

Craig Etheredge and I use the same words in separate phases, different words with the same meaning, and the same words with different meanings. I tease him that one day he will agree with me. Truthfully, we came to disciple-making as different types of leaders (groups guy and pastor) with a different starting point. You can enter the path at any phase. Walk the path, a long walk of obedience, and invite others to join you on the journey. **Start Small, Start Now.**

Start Groups Multiplication

Start Small: Pray for and enlist people who have a heart for other people.

Do It Right: Focus on Movement: Milk to Meat to Model.

Build It Strong: Send people out to create new groups: Mission to Multiply.

Disciple-Making Movement

Start Small: Pray for and invite three or four to join you.

Do It Right: Teach them to abide and obey.

Build It Strong: Send them to invite others to abide and obey.

YOUR OBSERVATIONS

1. As you have read, what is your Big Idea from this chapter?

2. What is the Bright Idea that has you thinking?

3. What is the Better Idea that you will implement?

CHAPTER 16

SECTION CLOSING THOUGHTS

...YOU TOO SHOULD BE GLAD AND REJOICE PHILIPPIANS 2:18

On the heels of sharing the Philippian Hymn of verses 6-11, Paul focuses on the results of abiding and obeying like Jesus. Paul modeled abiding and obeying for others that resulted in continuing the movement Jesus started. It also caused him to rejoice in the Spirit and prompt others to rejoice in making disciples who will make disciples until Jesus comes again.

Is your church in the pit, on a plateau, or at the pinnacle? Whatever situation you are in, you are called to make disciples who will make disciples for generations to come. Pastor, you are called to lead your church to become invested in the movement that Jesus began. If your church seems to be in conflict, then remind yourself what Jesus did when those in the "seat of Moses," were best described as a "brood of vipers." If your church is drifting, call and send them to the deep waters of discovering the call of Christ. If your church is on the rise, press on! Observe the things that Jesus did and imitate Him in all things for His glory. Regardless of where you are in the journey, I want to encourage you to

1. Start the movement in your church.

2. Start small by guiding a few to abide and obey.

3. Do it Right by modeling how to live by faith at home, at work, and wherever you go.

4. Build it Strong: abide in Him through prayer and the Word more than ever before in your life, obey Him because souls are at stake, and allow Him to build the Kingdom strong through you. His grace is sufficient…His power is made perfect in weakness…when I am weak, then I am strong" (2 Corinthians 12:9-10 NIV).

Eye-opening moment: I was blessed to have the opportunity to speak at the Evangelism Conference in Alaska. I asked for the privilege of working with a few local churches prior to the event. A pastor picked me up at 5:00 A.M. on Sunday morning to go to his church. We got an early start so that we could have breakfast before going to snowplow the church parking lot. On the way to the restaurant, the pastor shared how church members told him that you cannot do in Alaska what you can do in the lower forty-eight states. They said, "In Alaska, you cannot go up to a person and share the Gospel." The longer he talked, the more I realized that they had convinced him that was true. While we were eating, I noticed a man eavesdropping on our conversation. Instead of being annoyed, God helped me realize what was to happen. I invited the man to join us. He told us his story. I asked for the opportunity to share, and he agreed. God did a wonderful thing in his life and the life of the pastor that day. What you have observed Jesus do at the water fountains of life (John 4), you can do too. Observe and listen to Jesus. Great things will result.

CHAPTER 17

EPILOGUE

MY HOPE FOR YOU LUKE 10:20-21

The harvest is still plentiful. Pray to the Lord of the harvest, prepare like never before, and pray that you will care for the harvest He gives so that there will continue to be harvest days until He returns.

I want you to make disciples as described by the Great Commission of Matthew 28:19-20 and Acts 1:8. I hope you will disciple unto salvation (baptizing) and unto obedience. This means the movement must begin to include people beyond the walls of the local church. Guide disciples to share their faith testimony and a plan of salvation with those who do not know Christ. Equip your guides so that they will immediately begin to disciple these new converts. I hope you will guide them to see their Jerusalem, Judea, Samaria and ends of the earth mission field.

Finally, I hope you experience a Luke 10:21 "joy in the Spirit" like Jesus did when His disciples made disciples. I am weeping as I write these final words. I have long signed notes with one word, REJOICE! It does not come from Philippians 4:4, but from Luke 10:20. Why can we rejoice? Our names are written in Heaven! Make disciples who will make disciples, experience joy in the Spirit, and . . . ***REJOICE!***

Daniel

APPENDIX

RESOURCES

Take Scripture to HEART

Highlight: highlight words or verses that stand out to you.

Express: express why you highlighted the words or verses.

Ask: ask questions for clarity and understanding.

Relate: relate truth to life.

Tell: tell someone your next step.

Take Scripture to HEART

Highlight -

Express -

Ask -

Relate -

Tell -

Peter, James, and John Micro-group

Jesus called a group but had a group within the group that He spent time with apart from the others. Three men who would play instrumental roles in the future of disciple making: Peter, James, and John.

Why should you have Peter, James, and John?

Jesus did

Harvest principle

Guides that can be sent to start new groups

Application for today

Enlist-a Peter, James, and John micro-group to study with you (HEART)

Ask them to join you in increased participation with weekly assignments during group time

Model for them and encourage/equip them

Disciples Square: I do and you watch, I do and you help, You do and I help, You do and I watch, You do and teach

Over time they should be asked to enlist their own Peter, James, and John to prepare together

Increased participation, increased attendance, and increased guides

How I Prepare to Guide People

1. Pray with my group in mind
2. Read the passage in context
3. Use HEART as follows:
    a. Highlight
        i. What stands out to me
        ii. Words or phrases that merit definition for a new or non-believer
        iii. The most important phrase in the passage
    b. Express why it is important and prepare to explain everything highlighted
        i. Study trusted resources
        ii. If using curriculum refer to the teacher's guide
    c. Ask questions
        i. Ask questions addressed by the passage
        ii. Ask questions that members might ask
        iii. Ask questions that a non-believer might ask
        iv. Prepare to answer questions
    d. Relate truth to life
        i. How has it related to my life
        ii. How does it relate to everyone's life
    e. Tell someone
        i. Enlist a Peter, James, and John micro-group to study with me
        ii. Text them my insights and ask for their HEART information
        iii. Gradually enlist them to share at the appropriate time in the group
    f. Pray for wisdom, insight, and ability to guide the group
    g. Prepare to use opportunities tactfully to engage others in further study of questions surfaced in the group

Acts 1:8 Prayer List

Jerusalem: Family members and close friends

Judea: People in your community (where you live)

Samaria: People at work, school, etc. . . . (where you go each day)

Ends of Earth: Person X (people you encounter during the day)

Acts 1:8 Prayer List

Jerusalem: _____

Judea: _____

Samaria: _____

Ends of Earth: _____

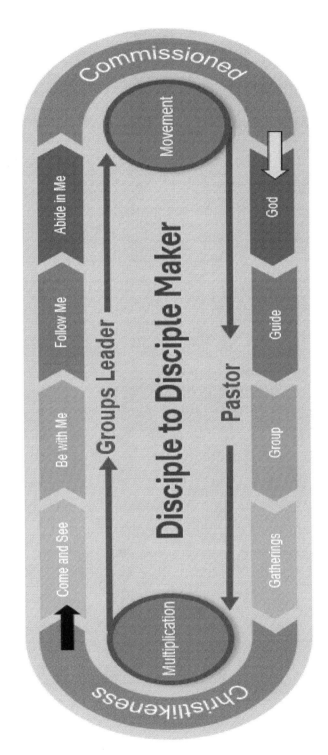

CONNECT:316

Connect:316 is a tool to develop a simple strategy to equip people to accomplish missional objectives.

Connect – Answers the *Why* question, for example, why do you need a group strategy? To CONNECT people to Christ, Community and Commission. Churches may change this word to fit their mission, vision, or core values.

316 – This number can be changed to reflect the church's context and/or emphasis. It does remind everyone of a key Scripture passage: John 3:16

3 – People – encourage and equip disciples to identify people who need connection to Christ, Community, or Commission.

1 – Plan/Path – encourage and equip disciples in the use of a plan, selected by leadership, that is designed to accomplish the connection objective. This number could change, but multiple paths could create confusion.

6 – Practices – encourage and equip disciples to utilize best practices in connecting people. Prayer should always be listed as the first practice.

CONNECT TO CHRIST, COMMUNITY, AND COMMISSION

CONNECT TO _____

PEOPLE:

_____

_____

_____

_____

_____

_____

_____

_____

PLAN: _____

PRACTICES: **PRAYER**

_____

_____

_____

_____

_____

_____

Bibliography

Adams, Ken. *Conversations About Disciple Making. Impact Discipleship Ministries.* 2019. p. 184.

Blackwell, Kevin, and Randy Norris. *Cultivate Disciplemaking. Make & Teach Discipleship Resources*, 2022. p. 168.

Bolsinger, Tod. *Canoeing the Mountains. IVP Books,* 2015. p. 247.

Breen, Mike. *Building a Discipling Culture. 3dm International,* 2017. p. 300.

Etheredge, Craig. *Bold Moves. discipleFIRST*, 2016. p. 240.

Etheredge, Craig. *The Disciple Making Leader. discipleFIRST*, 2022. p. 255.

Flake, Arthur. *The True Functions of a Sunday School, Convention Press.* 1930. p. 142.

Gainey, Mark C. *Disciple-Making Toolbox. Incite Publishing*, 2024. p. 148.

Gainey, Mark C. *4 Invitations. Incite Publishing*, 2021. p. 114.

Hyche, Larry. *First Letter: Basic Truths for a New Believer. Self-published, 2023. p. 72.*

Peterson, Eugene H. *A Long Obedience in the Same Direction: Discipleship in an Instant Society. IVP Books*, 2000. p. 216.

Phipps, Lawrence, and Daniel Edmonds. *Growing Sunday School/Small Group TEAMS. It's Life Ministry*, 1994. p. 45.

Phipps, Lawrence. *More Abundant Life. It's Life Ministry*, 2004. p. 208.

Sinek, Simon. *Start with Why. Portfolio/Penguin,* 2009. p. 246.

ABOUT THE AUTHOR

Daniel Edmonds has been a minister since 1981. Having served churches as a pastor and associate pastor with disciple-making responsibilities, he now serves the Alabama Baptist State Board of Missions as a State Missionary and functions as the Director of the Office of Sunday School & Discipleship.

Daniel has been a contributor and co-author of books and publications related to Sunday School and Disciple-making. He has partnered with numerous pastors and leaders to develop a pathway of disciple-making in the local church through a multiplying groups strategy and creating a movement of multiplying disciples.

As a five-year-old, his first job in Sunday School was chasing 'possums.

Made in the USA
Columbia, SC
22 September 2024

42763991R00076